# American Labor and the Law

**Bulletin of Comparative Labour Relations**

VOLUME 104

*Founding Editor*

The series started in 1970 under the dynamic editorship of Professor Roger Blanpain (Belgium), former President of the International Industrial Relations Association. Professor Blanpain, Professor Emeritus of Labour Law, Universities of Leuven and Tilburg, was also General Editor of the International Encyclopedia of Laws (with more than 1,600 collaborators worldwide) and President of the Association of Educative and Scientific Authors Authors. He passed away in October 2016.

*General Editor*

In 2015 Frank Hendrickx, Professor of labour law at the Faculty of Law of the University of Leuven (Belgium) joined as a co-Editor. Frank Hendrickx has published numerous articles and books and regularly advises governments, international institutions and private organisations in the area of labour law as well as in sports law. He is the Editor-in-Chief of the European Labour Law Journal and General Editor of the International Encyclopaedia of Laws.

*Introduction*

The Bulletins constitute a unique source of information and thought-provoking discussion, laying the groundwork for studies of employment relations in the 21st century, involving among much else the effects of globalization, new technologies, migration, and the greying of the population.

*Contents/Subjects*

Amongst other subjects the Bulletins frequently include the proceedings of international or regional conferences; reports from comparative projects devoted to salient issues in industrial relations, human resources management, and/or labour law; and specific issues underlying the multicultural aspects of our industrial societies.

*Objective*

The Bulletins offer a platform of expression and discussion on labour relations to scholars and practitioners worldwide, often featuring special guest editors.

*The titles published in this series are listed at the end of this volume.*

BULLETIN OF COMPARATIVE LABOUR RELATIONS – 104

# American Labor and the Law

## Dormant, Resurgent, and Emergent Problems

**Author**

Matthew W. Finkin



Wolters Kluwer

*Published by:*
Kluwer Law International B.V.
PO Box 316
2400 AH Alphen aan den Rijn
The Netherlands
E-mail: international-sales@wolterskluwer.com
Website: lrus.wolterskluwer.com

*Sold and distributed in North, Central and South America by:*
Wolters Kluwer Legal & Regulatory U.S.
7201 McKinney Circle
Frederick, MD 21704
United States of America
Email: customer.service@wolterskluwer.com

*Sold and distributed in all other countries by:*
Air Business Subscriptions
Rockwood House
Haywards Heath
West Sussex
RH16 3DH
United Kingdom
Email: international-customerservice@wolterskluwer.com

*Printed on acid-free paper.*

ISBN 978-94-035-0654-8

e-Book: ISBN 978-94-035-0655-5
web-PDF: ISBN 978-94-035-0660-9



Printed in the United Kingdom.

FSC
MIX
FSC® C103993

*I first met Roger Blanpain in the late 1980s when I was just getting my feet wet in the waters of comparative labor law. He was, I quickly learned, the "go to" figure in the field. The more immersed I became, the more our paths crossed—intertwined would be a better word. In an essay surveying the field a decade ago I described Roger as "the century's most indefatigable missionary for comparative labor law." And he was. He was also intellectually wide-ranging, persistently engaging and invariably provocative. It is a commonplace for a speaker giving a lecture of this sort to declare how privileged the speaker is by the invitation. In this case, the sentiment sheds the shopworn. I can only hope that what I am able to say will rise, if only in part, to the occasion of the presentation.*

# The Second Roger Blanpain Lecture

## The University of Leuven

## May 15, 2018

### About the Roger Blanpain Lectures:

This Bulletin contains the written version of the *Second Roger Blanpain Lecture*, delivered by Professor Matthew Finkin on May 15, 2018, at the Law Faculty of the University of Leuven.

The Roger Blanpain Lecture aims to bring a renowned expert in the field of labor law and labor relations to the Law Faculty of the KU Leuven once per year. The lecture series were initiated after the passing away of Professor Blanpain in 2016. The idea is to stay close to the academic approach of Professor Blanpain and the Leuven Institute for Labour Law, which implies the study of labor law from an international, comparative and cross-disciplinary perspective. The lecture aims to offer a 'window to the world' to our students and the Institute's academic and professional partners and friends.

Roger Blanpain (1932–2016) obtained his law degree at the University of Leuven, Belgium, where he also obtained his doctoral degree in 1956. In 1957, he obtained a master of arts degree from Columbia University, New York. At the Law Faculty of the University of Leuven, Blanpain held the chair in labor law until his retirement in 1998. As an emeritus professor, he continued teaching and publishing for many. His work had a strong international and comparative dimension. He saw the study of labor law and industrial relations as one and the same academic undertaking.

# Notes on Author

Matthew Finkin, Professor of Law, the University of Illinois, is the author of ten books and numerous scholarly publications; co-editor, *Comparative Labor Law & Policy Journal*; Dr. Dres. h.c. (U. of Trier and U. of Athens); holder, Humboldt Foundation Research Prize; *chevalier dans l'ordre des Palmes académiques*.

# Table of Contents

# Acknowledgments

I am indebted to the Institute of Advanced Studies, Nantes, France, an extended stay in which enabled me to commence upon a study of waged labor and the law of which this lecture is a part. A word of deep appreciation to the staff of the Albert E. Jenner, Jr. Memorial Law Library and especially Stephanie Davidson and Heather Simmons without whose help much that is set out here could not have been assembled. A final word of thanks to Sanford Jacoby for customarily acute comments toward the close.

# CHAPTER 1
# Introduction

The historian, Richard White, takes the year 1868 as the point at which the "American economy began its transition to large factories and wage labor."[1] The transition led to decades of intense struggle, often violent, sometimes fatal, over what came to be called "The Labor Question." Writ in upper case singular, The Labor Question tested the nature of citizenship in an economy no longer founded on yeomen farmers and independent artisans. Writ in lower case plural, labor's questions tested the role of law in addressing the contentious issues that mass waged labor generated. By the second quarter of the twentieth century, solutions—in hindsight, some partial and fragile—had been reached: citizenship would be redefined from independent proprietorship to market participation; laws would be fashioned to sand down the harsher edges of submission to market mediation and employer prerogative; collective workplace voice would find legal scaffolding.

Today, the Labor Question has recrudesced. Old issues have resurged, sometimes in altered guise. New issues have emerged. Both test the twentieth century's solutions.

What follows will sketch in those elements of the old order—economic, social, and ideological—that were challenged and then eclipsed by the rise to dominance of waged labor as a foundational element of American society. This will set the stage for an examination of "The Labor Question"—or questions—that so vexed the Republic. The solutions arrived at in the ensuing period of reform, after "long and grueling fights,"[2] will be laid on the page insofar as they found expression in law; some will be mentioned that have failed to attract attention, have yet to achieve political traction, are dormant. Against this background, labor's new questions—and a new Labor Question—will be posed.

1. Richard White, THE REPUBLIC FOR WHICH IT STANDS: THE UNITED STATES DURING RECONSTRUCTION AND THE GILDED AGE, 1865-1896, 817 (2017).
2. *Id.* at 526.

CHAPTER 2

# The Old Order

In the early decades of the nineteenth century, most of the work in America, done by husbands, wives, children, and mostly youthful "hired hands," was devoted to agriculture. Goods produced at home were sold to local merchants in what in Germany was called the *Kauf* system. Much was produced on the putting-out system, the *Verlagsstem*: raw materials, and not only for textile production, were given to homeworkers by merchants or factors who paid a piece rate for the finished product.[3] In 1840, the total value of household manufacture in the United States was over $29 million; this in a country with a population of seventeen million, or $1.70 of per capita value.[4] Farm ownership and home production, though subject to the vicissitudes of the weather and the market, were valued for the independence it seemed to offer. Without ignoring the often hardscrabble existence in the antebellum world, "Farmers, artisans, and merchants shared a sense of personal control over their fates in the old order because their work was governed either by the needs of their households or by personal interactions guided by custom and participants' reputations."[5]

3. *See, e.g.*, Thomas Dublin, *Women and Outwork in a Nineteenth-Century New England Town, Fitzwilliam, New Hampshire, 1830-1850 in* THE COUNTRYSIDE IN THE AGE OF CAPITALIST TRANSFORMATION 51 (Steven Hahn & Jonathan Prude eds. 1985); Jens Christensen & Peter Philips, *The Transition from Outwork to Factory Production in the Boot and Shoe Industry, 1830-1880 in* MASTERS TO MANAGERS: HISTORICAL AND COMPARATIVE PERSPECTIVES ON AMERICAN EMPLOYERS Ch. 1 (Sanford Jacoby ed. 1991); Christopher Clark, *Social Structures and Manufacturing Before the Factory: Rural New England*, 1750-1830 *in* THE WORKPLACE BEFORE THE FACTORY: ARTISANS AND PROLETARIANS, 1500-1800, 11, 30 (Thomas Safley & Leonard Rosenband eds. 1993) ("By the 1830s eighteen thousand women in Massachusetts were engaged in straw hatmaking alone; many thousands of others, there and in neighboring states, were engaged in making other goods for merchants. The rise of the Verlagssystem in New England accompanied, rather than preceded, the growth of the factory system.").
4. Rolla Milton Tryon, HOUSEHOLD MANUFACTURES IN THE UNITED STATES, 1640-1860, Table XVII at 308-309 (1917). Tryon points out that in 1819, New York appropriated $10,000 for the promotion of agriculture and family manufacture which was renewed for several years. *Id.* n. 2 at 306.
5. David Thelen, PATHS OF RESISTANCE: TRADITION AND DIGNITY IN INDUSTRIALIZING MISSOURI 13 (1986).

Finished goods, save those requiring significant capital investment such as iron manufacture, were produced in small artisanal workshops by a master, his wife and children, perhaps an apprentice, and one or more journeymen.[6] Journeymen had completed an apprenticeship and, though waged workers, they expected to accumulate enough capital to set themselves up as masters on their own. The status of journeyman, as a waged worker, was commonly thought to be only temporary, a way station to independence. Journeymen shared with their masters a "producer ideology" that maintained the value of "equality, citizenship, and especially independence," "an expectation that industrious apprentices and journeymen could achieve the goal of a 'competence' or independence as master mechanics."[7] Upward mobility occurred often enough before the Panic of 1837 to sustain the belief in proprietary independence as a foundational component of American society, for white male adults.[8] But wage labor as a permanent station in life was disreputable: it represented a state of "unmanly dependence," not all that far from slavery.[9] This sentiment took on added salience after the Civil War: "In the minds of most Northerners of the Civil War generation, democracy demanded independence, not only political, but economic."[10]

The ideology of producer independence played a role in antebellum labor protest as the expectation, even the hope of achieving independence became chimerical in many employments and receded in others. Journeymen struck against their masters

---

6. In 1820, before the boom following the construction of the Erie canal, most workers in Kingston, N.Y., lived in their employers' or masters' household. Stuart Blumin, THE URBAN THRESHOLD: GROWTH AND CHANGE IN A NINETEENTH CENTURY AMERICAN COMMUNITY 85-86 (1976).
7. L. Diane Barnes, ARTISAN WORKERS IN THE UPPER SOUTH: PETERSBURGH, VIRGINIA 1820-1865, 177-178 (2008) (references omitted). This was acutely felt in the South where white artisans were drawn into competition with skilled slave labor. In 1847, white workers struck the Tredegar Iron Works to demand the elimination of skilled slave labor. The strikers were fired. *Id.* at 108-109.
8. Billy Smith, *The Vicissitudes of Fortune: The Careers of Laboring Men in Philadelphia, 1750-1800* in WORK AND LABOR IN EARLY AMERICA 221, 250 (Stephen Innes ed. 1988) ("[O]n average, four of every ten journeymen shoemakers and tailors may have become independent each decade."); Stephen Ross, WORKERS ON THE EDGE: WORK, LEISURE, AND POLITICS IN INDUSTRIALIZING CINCINNATI, 1788-1870, 16 (1985) ("Traditional expectations of mobility through the trade from apprentice to journeyman to master persisted into the 1820s.")
9. Seth Rockman, SCRAPING BY: WAGE LABOR, SLAVERY, AND SURVIVAL IN EARLY BALTIMORE 241 (2009); Daniel Walker Howe, WHAT HATH GOD WROUGHT: THE TRANSFORMATION OF AMERICA, 1815-1848, 539 (2007). Textile mill-girls on strike in Lowell, Massachusetts, in 1836 sang,

> *Oh! Isn't it a pity, such a pretty girl as I, Should be sent to a factory to pine away and die. Oh! I cannot be a slave, I will not be a slave! For I'm so fond of liberty, That I cannot be a slave.*

*Quoted in* Chaim Rosenberg, CHILD LABOR IN AMERICA: A HISTORY 9 (2013) (italics in original).
10. Daniel T. Rogers, THE WORK ETHIC IN INDUSTRIAL AMERICA 1850-1920, 32 (1974). He notes, *inter alia*, that:

> The abolitionist Wendell Phillips, who before the war had dismissed the phrase "wages slavery" as "utterly unintelligible," by 1871 had joined a Massachusetts labor-reform convention in declaring "war" on the system of wages that cheated, demoralized, and "enslaved" the workingman. From close to the opposite end of the political spectrum, the *Nation*'s E.L. Godkin urged the agitation on "until the *régime* of wages, or, as we might perhaps better call it, the servile *régime*, has passed away as completely as slavery or serfdom."

when wage rates were reduced, their protest as much over workplace control as the wage itself.[11] Their demands were often expressed in terms infused with Republican ideology.[12] Between 1833 and 1836 a "wildfire" of strikes broke out, 172 by one count, including a general strike in 1835 of 20,000 workers in Philadelphia demanding the ten-hour day,[13] in effect, demanding that the workers take control of work time.[14] Women striking the Lowell, Massachusetts, mills in 1845, estimated at 2,000 in number, issued a proclamation declaring that they "remain in possession of our own unquestionable rights." "[A]s we are free, we would remain in possession of what kind Providence has bestowed upon us, and remain daughters of freemen still."[15] The women demanded to be recognized as "workers with legitimate rights to a fair and just wage for their labor, and citizens with legitimate rights to respectful treatment in the factory … ."[16] As Amy Dru Stanley observed,

---

11. Keepers of the Revolution: New Yorkers at Work in the Early Republic 69 (Paul Gilje & Howard Rock eds. 1992). In 1815, the Constitution of the Union Society of Shipwrights and Caulkers provided that they would work only for genuine and experienced shipbuilders, to keep out those who would cut wages by bringing in cheap labor. "If the shipwrights had to remain wage earners [as they had no expectation of becoming boatyard owners], they intended to have a say as to whom to accept as employers." *Id.* at 92. So, too, was a common protest over wage reductions that the masters acted unilaterally, and without bargaining with the journeymen. *See e.g.* the announcement of the Journeymen Cabinet Makers of New York City of December 22, 1802, *in* Howard Rock, The New York City Artisan 1789-1825: A Documentary History (1984) (Document No. 112 at 225). The common demand of organized journeymen was the retention of the power to determine their piece rates, that is their wages, which were, in practice, negotiated with the masters, as well as to limit the use of apprentices and women as cheap labor and to insist on the closed shop as a means of enforcing their rules. *See e.g.* Charles Steffen, The Mechanics of Baltimore: Workers and Politics in the Age of Revolution Ch. 10 (1984).
12. Gilje & Rock, *supra* n. 11, at 70. *See e.g.* "Carpenters' Strike Manifesto" (Apr. 10, 1809), *in* Rock, Documentary History, *supra* n. 11 at 234:

    > Among the unalienable rights of man are life, liberty, and the pursuit of happiness. By the social compact every class of society ought to be entitled to benefit in proportion to its usefulness, and the time and expense necessary to its qualification. Among the duties which individuals owe to society are single men to marry and married men to educate their children. Among the duties which society owes to individuals is to grant them compensation for services sufficient not only for the current expenses of livelihood, but to the formation of a fund for the support of that time of life when nature requires a cessation from labor. We will now revert to the particulars of our own situation, to show the justice and necessity of our demand.

13. Charles Sellers, The Market Revolution: Jacksonian America, 1815-1846, 338-339 (1991) (placing these events in the political context of the program and temporary success of the Working Mens Party); Howe, What Hath God Wrought, *supra* n. 9 at 548.
14. At the conclusion of a painstaking survey of the 1830s, Roediger and Foner conclude:

    > Because it so captured the imagination and aspirations of journeymen for full intellectual, political, and family life, and so clashed with the employer's desire for complete control over production, the ten-hour struggle evoked passionate commitment on both sides. Shorter hours were the focal point of the Jacksonian labor movement.

    David Roediger & Philip Foner, Our Own Time: A History of American Labor and the Working Day 41 (1989).
15. *Quoted in* David Zonderman, Aspirations & Anxieties: New England Workers & the Mechanized Factory System 1815-1850, 200-201 (1992).
16. *Id.*

> The stirring phrase "daughters of freemen" was also a warning about dangers of factory slavery and a clear rejection of bondage. These working women were forcefully stating that they were the descendants of free workers and citizens; they were not the slave children of slave parents.[17]

These tailors and cabinet makers, ships' caulkers and textile machine operatives demanded recognition of equality with their employers, their right to decent wages and reasonable hours, to a degree of control of their working lives. These efforts do not suggest that waged labor was seen as the gateway to citizenship, but rather that means had to be found to accommodate the permanence of wage labor within a framework of citizenship.

A demographic turning point was reached in 1868. Census data after the Civil War indicated that "for the first time in the nation's history wage earners had come to outnumber the self-employed, a situation contradicting ideals of economic independence; and the disproportion grew larger over time."[18] The shift from artisanal manufacture to mass factory production, from skilled to semi-skilled labor, often immigrant and female, from small proprietary enterprise to huge vertically integrated corporations would challenge the assumption that wage labor was compatible with the Republic's understanding of citizenship.

17. Amy Dru Stanley, FROM BONDAGE TO CONTRACT: WAGE LABOR, MARRIAGE, AND THE MARKET IN THE AGE OF SLAVE EMANCIPATION 62 (1998).
18. *Id.* at 60.

CHAPTER 3

# "The Country That We Once Knew Is Not Now Known to Us"

In 1850, the population of the U.S. above the age of ten stood at about 16.5 million of whom fewer than half were in the labor market.[19] In 1870, the population was over 29 million, and most of the working age population was engaged in waged labor: 52.5% of those over 10 years of age worked in agriculture; 19% in manufacturing; 11.5% in trade and various services.[20] The size of employing enterprises was to grow significantly.[21] Between 1870 and 1910 agricultural employment fell to 31%—to fall to 1.1% in 2009. Blue collar jobs in manufacturing, mining, construction, transportation and the like constituted over 38% of the labor market in 1910. Beginning in the 1880s, industry embarked on a massive shift toward vertical integration which, as Alfred

19. John Swinton, A MOMENTOUS QUESTION: THE RESPECTIVE ATTITUDES OF CAPITAL AND LABOR 36 (1895). Swinton (1830-1901) was editor of *John Swinton's Paper,* termed by Selig Perlman "the best labor paper in the country's history." Selig Perlman, *Swinton, John,* in 14 ENCYCLOPEDIA OF THE SOCIAL SCIENCES 491 (Edwin R.A. Seligman ed. 1934).
20. The data are set out in Robert Gordon, THE RISE AND FALL OF AMERICAN GROWTH, Table 8-1 at p. 255 (2016).
21. Bruce Lurie & Mark Schmitz take Philadelphia in the period 1850-1880 as a prime example of a highly diversified labor market. They lay out the percentage distribution of employment by firm size in Philadelphia in that period.

| *Firms* | *1850* | *1880* |
|---|---|---|
| 1-5 employees | 12.4% | 7.0% |
| 6-25 employees | 28.4% | 15.1% |
| 26-50 employees | 16.1% | 11.9% |
| 50+ employees | 43% | 65.0% |

Bruce Lurie & Mark Schmitz, *Manufacture and Productivity: The Making of an Industrial Base, Philadelphia, 1850-1880* in PHILADELPHIA: WORK, SPACE, FAMILY, AND GROUP EXPERIENCE IN THE 19TH CENTURY 43, Table 5 at 52 (Theodore Hershberg ed. 1981).

Chandler has shown, was fully evolved by the 1920s.[22] By 1919, more than 70% of manufacturing workers in the U.S. worked for firms employing more than 100 workers, more than a quarter for firms employing more than 1,000.[23] In sum, a country composed of small farmers and proprietors a century before now rested predominantly on the employment of semi-skilled blue collar workers in mass production industries.

Thus was the stage set for a decades-long struggle with "The Labor Question."[24] To some, the question was singular: How to sustain a democracy that had come to rest on a polity the majority of whose productive members are in a state of what had long been thought to be near servility? In 1868, John Orvis, prominent in labor reform since 1848, "[e]choing other writers of the post war period" put it thusly, "'[T]he labor question ... is the question of Reconstruction come North .... It means the deliverance, exaltation, and ennobling of labor and the laboring classes.'"[25] The question was put that way with ever greater urgency in the wake of protests and strikes, injunctions and violence including the use of federal troops as well as deputized private police at and after the century's turn. Put that way, the answer could be equally singular, in calls for the abandonment of the capitalist order. In 1869, the Noble Order of the Knights of Labor, a "distinctly American phenomenon,"[26] was founded, destined to a spectacular rise and an equally spectacular fall. It had one foot in the old order, wedded to the producerist ideal, and the other foot in, and even in advance of the new order[27]: it admitted to membership skilled craftsmen and unskilled workers, shopkeepers and editors, blacks and whites, men and women—but not lawyers. It was dedicated to the

22. Alfred Chandler, THE VISIBLE HAND: THE MANAGERIAL REVOLUTION IN AMERICAN BUSINESS Ch. 11 (1977).
23. U.S. Bureau of Census, ABSTRACT OF THE FOURTEENTH CENSUS, 1920 Table 15 at p. 998-99 (1923).
24. The Labor Question emerged among a host of other issues that consumed the public as American society rushed headlong toward a different social order: the "land question," that swept in both the plight of tenant farmers and Henry George's single tax movement; the "money question," of the gold standard, "free silver" or fiat currency; the "Negro question," of equal political, economic, and social rights for freedmen; the "women's question," centering on suffrage but that included women's role in the workplace; and a good deal more.
25. *Quoted in* David A. Zonderman, UNEASY ALLIES: WORKING FOR LABOR REFORM IN NINETEENTH CENTURY BOSTON 126 (2011). *See also* Washington Gladden, THE LABOR QUESTION 90 (1911) ("the question is whether we are ready to see our democracy complete itself."); Richard T. Ely, STUDIES IN THE EVOLUTION OF INDUSTRIAL SOCIETY (461) (1903)("The question is this, Is our social order essentially sound, has it vitality and capacity for improvement, or is it essentially unsound so that it must give way to anew social order?").
26. Mary R. Beard, *Knights of Labor* in 8 ENCYCLOPAEDIA OF THE SOCIAL SCIENCES 581, 582 (Edwin R.A. Seligman, ed. 1932).
27. Edwin Gabler put the context thusly,

> The Gilded Age labor movement had a refreshing open-endedness that the Knights mirrored. Look through the pages of *John Swinton's Paper* in the mid-1880s and find Greenbackers, German socialists, Single Taxers, pure-and-simple men, Irish Land Leaguers, and Knights as peaceable neighbors in the journal's columns. What this lacked in uniformity it made up for in variety and wholesome debate. Currents of reform and activism overlapped and interacted, and probably nowhere so much as in the Knights of Labor.

Edwin Gabler, THE AMERICAN TELEGRAPHER: A SOCIAL HISTORY, 1869-1900, 193 (1988) (reference omitted). *See also* the discussion of the amalgam of "past and present" in the Knights' movement, *id.* at pp. 198-201.

abolition of wage labor and the creation of a co-operative commonwealth even as it made common cause with trade unions.[28]

The role of unions was fought out not only in the workplace but in public opinion as well. Illustration 1, an anti-union cartoon of the Gilded Age, artfully appeals to the worker's independence, not from the employer but from the union at a time when the "closed shop," which required union membership in order to get or hold a job, was a *sine qua non* of union representation.

28. Leon Fink, Workingmen's Democracy: The Knights of Labor in American Politics 23 (1983) (reprinting the Knights' founding *Declaration of Principles*).

**Illustration 1**

An anti-union cartoon of the Gilded Age. The "walking delegate," a term first used in 1886, described a union agent who visited workplaces to see that union rules and agreements were observed. The stereotype of the silk-hatted "walking delegate" enriching the union at the expense of oppressed workers was common in anti-union propaganda at the time and had a persuasive effect on public opinion. Robert Brooks, WHEN LABOR ORGANIZES 79 (1937).

As the century progressed, the call for the abolition of wage labor was heard across a spectrum of radical movements: anarchist, socialist, syndicalist, communist.[29] Some, by no means indifferent to the "storm" of "labor troubles" accompanying the rise of "great manufacturing centers with their crowds of operatives, their strikes, their lockouts and boycotts,"[30] saw The Labor Question from a broader perspective. To Henry Booth, it was rooted in the replacement of labor by machines:

> The term *labor-saving* machinery is not a misnomer, but conveys the correct idea. It means machinery which saves labor, or dispenses with the services of the laborer.
>
> This, then, is the revolution which we are called upon to face ... .[31]

If work was to become the measure of the citizen, what is to be done if there were to be an insufficiency of work? This, John Swinton opined in 1895, was "*the* most serious problem that has ever confronted mankind": the displacement of labor (albeit only "manual labor") by "new mechanical appliances."[32] His perception was anticipated when, in 1876, the Boston Eight Hour League's annual convention was held under a banner that read, "Machinery is discharging *labor*, faster than new employments are provided." [33] As Rosanne Currarino has pointed out, such was a prominent and recurring view at the time of what The Labor Question was.[34]

To others, however, the question was plural, not singular. As much could be said in Europe struggling with what there was called the "Social Question." In 1881, Léon Gambetta gave an after-dinner speech in which he drew attention to France's industrial

29. The literature on these various radical movements is simply enormous. One ought also to note the People's Party, which had a spectacular rise in 1892 and an equally spectacular collapse in the wake of the 1896 elections. Its platform called for the government ownership of the railroads and utilities, for land redistribution, and collective bargaining. *See generally*, POPULISM: THE CRITICAL ISSUES (Sheldon Hackney ed. 1971). Mention ought also be made of The Industrial Workers of the World—the "Wobblies"—founded in Chicago in 1905. It's constitution, amended in 1908, proclaimed:

> The working class and the employing class have nothing in common. There can be no peace so long as hunger and want are found among millions of working people and the few, who make up the employing class, have all the good things of life.
>
> Between these two classes a struggle must go on until the workers of the world organize as a class, take possession of the earth and the machinery of production, and abolish the wage systems.

*Quoted in* Eldridge Dowell, A HISTORY OF CRIMINAL SYNDICALISM LEGISLATION IN THE UNITED STATES 26 (1939).

30. Henry Booth, *The Labor Question*, 1 Chicago Law Times 11, 12 (1887). Booth, about 70 at the time of this speech, was a former judge and Dean of the Union College of Law in Chicago, predecessor of the School of Law of Northwestern University. A contemporary describes him as a laborer for social improvement. James Babb, *Union College of Law*, 1 The Green Bag 330, 331 (1889).
31. Booth, *The Labor Question*, *supra* n. 30 at 15 (italics in original).
32. Swinton, A MOMENTOUS QUESTION, *supra* n. 19 at 18-19 (emphasis added).
33. *Quoted in* Zonderman, UNEASY ALLIES *supra* n. 25 at 145-146 (italics in original).
34. Rosanne Currarino, THE LABOR QUESTION IN AMERICA: ECONOMIC DEMOCRACY IN THE GILDED AGE 15, 25, 26, 29 (2011). This issue was set out as part of the *Manifesto of the International Working Peoples' Association* reprinted in Richard T. Ely, THE LABOR MOVEMENT IN AMERICA 358, 359 (1886) (no date given).

problems, "which I have always refused to call 'the social question'. And, gentlemen, do you know why? It is because when one studies society carefully, analytically ... one realizes that one can only resolve these problems one at a time, with the power of study, with goodwill and above all with the force of knowledge and hard work."[35]

Labor's questions commanded public attention at and in the decades immediately following the century's turn as a result of the extraordinary depth and violence accompanying labor disputes, disputes often as much over the legitimacy of worker representation as over the issues their unions sought to resolve: the Pullman strike of 1894, which shut down the nation's western railroads in which more than thirty workers were killed in street fights in Chicago and to quell the U.S. army occupied the city; the Ludlow Massacre of 1914, in which seven strikers, two striker's wives and eleven of their children were killed in an assault on their camp—as they had been evicted from company housing; the two coalfield wars in West Virginia—1912-18 and 1919-21—the former triggering a declaration of martial law, the latter pitting nine thousand armed miners against the coal company's armed guards and civil authority in their pay, quelled by federal troops; to name but a few.

These various threads of thought came lightly bound together with the advent of the Great Depression in which the very future of capitalism seemed to be at stake, when the threat—or promise—of radicalism seemed very real. At that time, two books by academic economists—E.E. Cummins and Carroll Daugherty—appeared that surveyed the terrain. They presented identical accounts of labor's problems that posed issues of public policy. As they saw it, these were:

| *The Labor Problem*[36] | *Labor Problems*[37] |
|---|---|
| unemployment | unemployment |
| work hours | work hours |
| industrial accident & injury | industrial accident & injury |
| insecurity | Insecurity |

35. Discours et Plaidoyers Politiques de M. Gambetta 122-23 (1883):

> Mais il y a une ... tâche qui nous sollicite et qui s'impose à nous, c'est ce que j'appelle la solution des problèms économiques et industriels, et ce que je me refuserai toujours à appeler la question sociale; et savez-vous pourquoi, Messieurs? C'est parce que quand on étudie la société, plus on l'examine, plus on l'analyse, plus on la fouille, plus on étudie le passé dont nous sommes sortis ... alors on constate qu'on ne peut résoudre ces problems qu'un à un, à force, d'études et de bonne volonté, et surtout à force de connaissances et de labeurs.

The reporter indicates that these remarks—given at a banquet of the commercial association of retail wine merchants of Paris—were met with lively approval ("*vive approbation*"). Léon Gambetta (1818-1882), a politician of the left, was briefly Prime Minister before his death.

36. E.E. Cummings, The Labor Problem in the United States (2d ed. 1935).
37. Carroll R. Daugherty, Labor Problems in American Industry (1933).

| *The Labor Problem*[36] | *Labor Problems*[37] |
|---|---|
| wages and income | wages and income |
| | "substandard workers"[38] |

There are subtle distinctions in treatment. Daughterty, for example, separately treats problems particular to low-wage workers: the persistence of forced labor among blacks in the south, in logging and turpentine camps; wage garnishment; and wage theft, that is "the *occasional* inability of the worker to collect from his employer the wages actually earned."[39] But, the lion's share of both books is taken up with labor disputes and employee representation. In the 1930s, this *was* The Labor Question.

Before reaching it, it is noteworthy that the common concern in both about wages was expressed not only in the workers' ability to maintain a standard of living but also in the distribution of income in the economy. Both Cummins and Daugherty attended to the distribution of household wealth, which includes more than earned income. But Cummins, relying on a study taken from income tax data, did attend to the distribution of earned income which, for the vast majority of wage workers, would only be the wages they earned. The figures he came up with can be compared with the distribution earnings in 2010, set out in Table 3.1.

*Table 3.1 Comparative Distribution of Earned Income 1918 & 2010*

| | *1918* | *2010* |
|---|---|---|
| Top 1% | 14% | 17.2% |
| Bottom 90% | 65% | 55% |

*Source*: For 1918: National Bureau of Economic Research, 1 INCOME IN THE UNITED STATES 134-35 (1922). For 2010, Lawrence Mishel, Josh Bevins, Elise Gould & Heidi Shierholz, THE STATE OF WORKING AMERICA Table 6.1 at p. 379 (12th ed. 2012).

The distribution of wealth was of concern because of the relationship of wealth to opportunity, to social mobility. Daugherty dwelt at greater length on the social repercussions, aware of the repression of labor unrest and the suppression of civil liberties that had occurred and was even then occurring:

> Wealth often enables its owners to block legislation which might help to equalize opportunity and income. It frequently enables them to dominate political parties, conventions, and elections .... The uneven distribution of income often prevents wage earners from giving to their children the education and training which would develop their native capacities .... The "civil liberties" of freedom of speech and assemblage are too often curtailed by wealth-dominated police and militia. Through all these things the owners of wealth tend to perpetuate their power, and

38. Today, the caption would surely be headed, "substandard work" or "working conditions" for those he treats: children, women, casual labor, black labor, convict labor, and southern labor.
39. Daugherty, *supra* n. 37, at 202 (emphasis added).

> the net result is a decided repression upon any opposing forces which might tend to democratize opportunity and broaden the possession of wealth and income.[40]

Those who sought legal answers to labor's questions faced two features of the American legal scene that channeled and constrained their efforts. The first was structural. Until the New Deal revolution of the 1930s, the U.S. Supreme Court had limited the ability of Congress to legislate under its constitutional power over foreign and interstate commerce. The federal government could not enact labor legislation save for those employees whose work actually took them across a state border. This limited federal labor law almost exclusively to maritime and interstate railroad workers and truckers. As a result, it fell to the states to become laboratories for the production of labor law. After federal constitutional power expanded as a result of Supreme Court decisions in the 1930s, Congress could draw on those and future state efforts in fashioning national labor law; and it did.

The second was ideological. Before the Civil War, slavery's defenders extolled its paternalism in counterpoint to the harsh realities of what they termed "wage slavery" in the North. Defenders of "free labor" fell back on a key distinction: waged workers had freedom of contract; slaves did not. By century's end, the courts transformed what was a proposition of fact into a fortress of constitutional principle—"freedom of contract" —that advocates had to surmount in order to sustain the constitutionality of labor protective legislation, laws that defeated the market and constrained contract terms. Advocates for labor law argued that deference to contractual freedom required a relationship of economic equality which was absent for workers facing huge corporations. But, for decades, the courts, state as well as federal, resisted that proposition even as it became more and more obvious to everyone else.[41] As Richard White put it, "The courts opened the gates of the judicial fortress, beckoned the politically defeated in, and guarded them with a set of aging, discredited, and rejected beliefs that now rested mostly on judicial authority."[42] The Supreme Court was later to reflect back on these decisions as based on judicially "self-mesmerized views of economic and social theory."[43] As we will see, some of what the Court is doing today resurrects that mindset to analogous effect, but that is for treatment later on.

Suffice it to say at this point, in the aftermath of the New Deal, the fortress of economic due process, by then sapped by concessions to the exercise of public power

40. Daugherty, *supra* n. 37, at 204.
41. As Rep. Schneider put it in the debate on the law to deny enforcement of "yellow dog" contracts, agreements that restricted the capacity of employees to engage in concerted action or to join unions:

> This [freedom-of-contract] doctrine presupposes that the girl who seeks a position in a department store, and the owner of that store deal with each other on terms of equality. She is free to work or not to work; he is free to employ or not to employ her.
>
> Or ... that a worker seeking employment with the United States Steel Corporation and the manager, acting for the corporation, deal on terms of equality. One who still believes that will believe anything.

75 Cong. Rec. 5515 (Mar. 8, 1932) (remarks of Rep. Schneider).
42. White, The Republic for Which It Stands, *supra* n. 1 at 822.
43. Bhd. of R.R. Trainmen v. Jacksonville Terminal Co., 394 U.S. 369, 382 (1969).

for limited labor protective purposes,[44] fell. The courthouse door opened wide to the enforcement of labor protective law at both the state and federal levels. However, at that time as before, the courts struggled to apply a common law rooted in an agrarian society of independent proprietors to the circumstances of an industrial world. The law's course in two particular aspects that could have contemporary resonance is sketched in below.

44. David Currie, *The Constitution and the Supreme Court: The Protection of Economic Interests*, 1889-1910, 52 U. Chi. L. Rev. 324 (1985).

# CHAPTER 4
# The Law's Course

## §4.01 FROM EARLY INDUSTRIALIZATION THROUGH THE GILDED AGE

### [A] Labor Legislation and the Charting of New Paths

Massachusetts was the early seat of factory production, most importantly in textiles, and became the first mover as well in labor protective legislation. By the mid-1840s, Massachusetts had enacted laws limiting child labor, regulating the work hours of women and children, assuring the safety of dangerous industrial appliances—boilers and engines—and providing for factory inspection.[45] Other states followed.

Over the ensuing half century more labor protections were legislated, often with almost pointillistic precision to deal with a specific evil in a specific employment.[46] Several states, for example, mandated that seating be made available to workers who had to stand for long periods of time, such as trolly car drivers, and sometimes had additionally to legislate that these employees actually be allowed to use them.[47] Laws

---

45. Charles Persons, Mabel Parton & Maybelle Moses, LABOR LAWS AND THEIR ENFORCEMENT WITH SPECIAL REFERENCE TO MASSACHUSETTS (Susan Kingsburg ed. 1911).
46. In 1896, Carroll Wright, the U.S. Commissioner of Labor, compiled a compendium of all the labor legislation in the U.S. It consumed 1,357 pages. U.S. Bureau of Labor, LABOR LAWS OF THE UNITED STATES (1896).
47. New Jersey law provided that,

> All horse car passenger railroads in the cities and towns of this State shall provide a proper seat upon the front platform of each car, for the use of the driver on such car when driving the same, under reasonable restrictions by the company operating such car as to the use of the said seat in going up or down grade or otherwise.

Set out *id.* at p. 682. Such was an issue not only for street car drivers but also for women in retail sales. Susan Porter Benson, COUNTER CULTURES: SALESWOMEN, MANAGERS, AND CUSTOMERS IN AMERICAN DEPARTMENT STORES, 1890-1940, 140 (1986). New Jersey dealt with both. LABOR LAWS OF THE UNITED STATES at p. 681. These laws continue to be of relevance. *See* Kilby v. CVS Pharmacy, Inc., 368 P.3d 554 (Cal. 2016).

addressed similarly specific issues: safety in mining, railroading, and manufacture; laborers' wage liens in construction—note the echo here of the producerist ethic; tenement manufacture, inspection, and licensure; strikes and boycotts; and more. Overarching all, the law confronted worker death and dismemberment on an industrial scale and responded in the creation of worker compensation systems.

The law and literature on the most controversial and far-reaching of these measures—job safety and worker compensation—enormous.[48] These areas have largely receded from the stage to the wings of modern labor's problems. But two of these early legislative engagements are worthy of note: child labor and lead contractor wage liability. The path they took anticipates the metamorphosis of labor questions a century on; they placed potentially usable precedents on the page.

### *[1] Child Labor: Identifying the Employer*

Child labor would seem to be an odd choice for contemporary relevance. Children had been put to work since antiquity; their presence at work was little noticed let alone criticized in until the advent of the factory.[49] Pressure for reform grew apace in the Gilded Age driven by humanitarian concerns[50] as children came to be employed in large numbers in coal mining, textile manufacture, glass bottle production, cigar and garment tenement manufacture, in "street trades" as newsboys, messengers, and buskers (often incited by parents). Reform efforts resulted in a complex web of state laws of highly variable content and impact, as enforcement was near-universally problematic.[51] Given the constrained reach of the commerce clause that disallowed a federal child labor law, in 1924 Congress passed an amendment to the constitution that would have allowed for the enactment of child labor legislation, but the necessary number of states refused to agree.[52] In 1938, Congress passed the Fair Labor Standards Act which provided a uniform floor for the regulation of child labor, the constitutionality of which figured in the Supreme Court's abandonment of its constrained view of the commerce power. It would seem accordingly that this particular labor question has been settled; there is scant public pressure today to do more in the matter of child labor.

48. Two recent studies supply a good introduction. John Fabian Witt, The Accidental Republic: Crippled Workingmen, Destitute Widows, and the Remaking of American Law (2004) and Donald Rogers, Making Capitalism Safe: Work Safety and Health Regulation in America, 1880-1940 (2009).
49. James Schmidt, Industrial Violence and the Legal Origins of Child Labor 43-47 (2010).
50. Such was described as the motive force by John Commons & John Andrews, Principles of Labor Legislation 24-27 (1916).
51. These laws are compiled by Hannah Sewall, Child Labor in the United States (Bureau of Labor Bull. No. 52) (May 1904).
52. Alain Grimes, Democracy and the Amendments to the Constitution 101-104 (1978). Congressional opposition centered largely on the infringement of the states' right to regulate child labor—or not, as they chose. Some critics saw the measure as "part of a hellish scheme laid in foreign countries to destroy our Government. Many of the proponents of the measure are communists and socialists." 65 Cong. Rec. 10122 (June 2, 1924) (remarks of Sen. Stephens); and Senator Dial: "This is the first step to unemployment compensation … . Socialism is rapidly overtaking us." *Id.* at 10119 (remarks of Sen. Dial).

Nonetheless, there is something more, something worthy of consideration in the context of the twenty-first century's labor problems. Before reaching that, however, there is room as well to rethink the role of humanitarianism as the singular motive force for legal reform. The depiction of children, sometimes quite young, caught in the maw of industrial production, captured in photographs,[53] literature, and the press outraged the middle class and triggered demands for reform; but more was involved. Thomas Haskell has argued that the capitalist market economy, as it arose in eighteenth-century England and flourished in nineteenth-century America, taught market participants to think causally, not only about their short-term transactions but "to attend to the remote consequences" of them.[54] (Immanuel Wallerstein reminds us that the capitalist system bases profit on the deferral of realized value.[55]) This manner of thought came to dominate a market-driven economy and politics. Demands to reform the institution of child labor were bound up in demands for public schooling[56]: with a concern not only for what an eight-year old "glass house boy" in bottle manufacture will do when he becomes an adult and is no longer needed for the only work he knows,[57] but what kind of society will emerge when a significant segment of the population consists of educationally stunted adults with scant prospects in the labor market.[58] If labor market participation and not independent proprietorship was to characterize citizenship, it followed that children—not yet adults, not yet full citizens—should be excluded from the market while being prepared for their future, adult role.

That having been said, a feature of many of these child labor laws that could retain relevance today treats the determination of the person or entity responsible for these laws' observance. A study has addressed the issue for this very purpose with a textured discussion of the legal history of the obliviousness of the law of child and, at points, female labor to the existence of a proximate common law employment relationship.[59] Even as it draws on roots in criminal law, British and American, less space is devoted to that which is of interest here—the legal status of the worker as a minor.

Unemancipated minors lacked contractual capacity. At common law, a contract of employment made by an unemancipated minor was voidable; that is, the minor could disclaim it and demand compensation on the basis of the value of the work

53. Some are displayed in Chaim Rosenberg's, CHILD LABOR IN AMERICA: A HISTORY (2013).
54. Thomas Haskell, *Capitalism and the Origins of the Humanitarian Sensibility, Part 2*, 90 Am. Hist. Rev. 547, 561 (1985).
55. Immanuel Wallerstein, 1 THE MODERN WORLD SYSTEM 46 (1974).
56. Schmidt, *supra* n. 49 at 45-46.
57. James Flannery, THE GLASS HOUSE BOYS OF PITTSBURGH: LAW, TECHNOLOGY, AND CHILD LABOR (2009). A glass house clerk observed in a 1907-1908 survey, "What becomes of them, do you say, by the time they are twenty-two or twenty-three? The workhouse. They are no good to us anymore." Flannery treats the relationship of school laws to child labor legislation in Ch. 5.
58. These longer-term social implications were prefigured in the eighteenth century debate on whether the U.S. should industrialize at all and the sort of citizenry that would populate the New Republic if it did. THE PHILOSOPHY OF MANUFACTURES: EARLY DEBATES OVER INDUSTRIALIZATION IN THE UNITED STATES (Michael Folsom & Steven Luba reds. 1982).
59. Bruce Goldstein, Marc Linder, Laurence Norton, II & Catherine Ruckelshaus, *Enforcing Fair Labor Standards in the Modern American Sweatshop: Rediscovering the Statutory Definition of Employment*, 46 UCLA L. Rev. 983, 1015-1055 (1999) [hereinafter Goldstein et al.].

performed.[60] This created an obvious and unacceptable zone of legal uncertainty for employers. One solution was for the employer to contract with the father for the child's labor. The father, who had a right at common law to the services of his children, could assign that right to a third party, the child's wages to be paid to the father.[61] When this device was resorted to, child labor became a tripartite relationship.

A more creative and direct solution was devised: to treat the child's entering employment as working a partial emancipation implied by law.[62] Some states took this approach legislatively, by providing that wages would be paid to the child unless the parent notified the employer that the child's wages should be paid to the parent.[63]

A second feature of the workplace at the time that further complicated the enforcement of child labor restrictions was the use of subcontracting, either in a clearly defined, structured, industrial relationship—in which the "inside contractor" functioned as a proprietor[64]—or the more informal allowance of overseers and even workers to employ helpers on their own account, often children as in textile manufacture and mining.[65] In the case of contracting with a father, the company was an assignee. In the case of subcontracting, the subcontractor was the employer, which created no little confusion for those child labor prohibitions that required only those who "hire or employ" to observe the law's strictures.[66] Some statutes dealt with the problem by having their child labor laws apply to any persons who "employs or permits [a child] to be employed."[67] But other states legislated even more aggressively, extending the law to those who "suffer or permit [a child] to work."[68]

60. The texture of case law on contractual capacity and its nuances when it comes to parental rights and contracting is dense. The law of child employment is summarized in one volume by H.G. Wood, A TREATISE ON THE LAW OF MASTER AND SERVANT § 3 at 12-14 (2d ed. 1886), and set out in an eight volume work, C.B. Labatt, COMMENTARIES ON THE LAW OF MASTER AND SERVANT (1913), in which the issue is treated in greater detail in § 99 at pp. 353-355 of Volume I.
61. Labatt, *supra* n. 60, § 636 at 1813.
62. *Id.*, § 647 at pp. 1832-1837. *See, e.g.*, Tennessee Manuf. Co. v. James, 18 S.W. 262 (Tenn. 1892). The law's historical setting is explored by James Schmidt, *supra* n. 49 at 128-135.
63. These are set out in Hannah Sewall, *supra* n. 51. Iowa and Washington forbade a parent from recovering a wage that had been paid to the child.
64. *See* John Buttrick, *The Inside Contract System*, 12 J. Econ. Hist. 205 (1952) and Ernest Englander, *The Inside Contract System of Production and Organization: A Neglected Aspect of the History of the Firm*, 28 Labor Hist. 429 (1987). From the 1850s to 1877, railroads had experimented with inside contractors even to the running of the trains. Walter Licht, WORKING FOR THE RAILROAD: THE ORGANIZATION OF WORK IN THE NINETEENTH CENTURY 19-24 (1983). As Walter Licht explains of the proponents of contracting: "Embodied in their proposals was a ... . Jeffersonian vision of an American nation of autonomous producers and citizens." *Id.* at 24.
65. Schmidt discusses the loose practices in Southern industries of the time, *supra* n. 49 at 178-180.
66. These included Colorado, Florida, Pennsylvania, and South Carolina. *See* Sewall, *supra* n. 51.
67. *E.g.* Alaska, Indiana, and Rhode Island, *in* Sewall, *supra* n. 51.
68. According to the laws as of 1896 reprinted by Hannah Sewall, *supra* n. 51, these included: Alabama, Arkansas, Illinois, Indiana, Maryland, New Jersey, New York, and Washington. Starting in 1910, the National Conference of Commissioners on Uniform State Laws embarked upon an effort to draft a uniform child labor law. The Commissioners surveyed the scene of extant law and adopted the formula of "suffer or permit" to work; but, they did not examine the provenance of the phrase, why it read as it did. PROCEEDINGS OF THE TWENTIETH ANNUAL CONFERENCE OF THE COMMISSIONERS ON UNIFORM STATE LAWS (1910).

It is a perplexing turn of phrase. To "suffer" usually means to "allow," that is, to "permit." If this is what "to suffer" was intended to mean, the addition of "permit" would do no work, it would be surplusage, a practice disfavored in legislative drafting. But to "suffer" also means to "tolerate." Maryland's prohibition on child labor applied to any person who "suffered or permitted" such child labor but, unlike other states, Maryland went on to define the term: "The word 'suffer or permit,' includes every act or omission, whereby it becomes *possible* for the child to engage in such labor."[69] Employment of the child by the enterprise to be held responsible was not required.[70]

The phrase was adopted in the federal Fair Labor Standards Act of 1938 which applied it not only to the law's treatment of child labor but also to the law's wage and hour provisions. The clause has been read by the U.S. Supreme Court as requiring the most expansive approach to deciding whether an entity is a worker's employer, by an examination of the "economic reality" of the relationship.[71] However so expansive, the governing factors applied by the Court play into the person's economic dependence on the ostensible employer not whether, even by some act or omission, the person or business has made the violation possible, even if only by tolerating the person's presence in the workplace or role in the performance of the work. That would seem to be the original intent of the definition. Read that way, the provision could have far-reaching consequences in the structure of modern enterprise, as will be seen.

### *[2] Wage Liability up Contracting Chains*

One significant labor law reform sought at the time, one that resonated strongly with the ideal of proprietary independence, was to give workers on construction projects a lien for their unpaid wages against the property they worked on.[72] However, these laws, modeled on the mechanic's lien, applied to "the whole or a part of the property of persons *for whom* the work ... is performed."[73]

69. Md. Code Art. 27, § 219 (1903) (emphasis added) *reprinted in* Hannah Sewall, *supra* n. 51 at 588. The provenance of the Maryland provision is discussed by Goldstein et al., *supra* n. 59 at 1031-1032. They also discuss the case law of the extension of "suffer and permit" to the use of children by independent contractors who did work on the employer's premises, *e.g.* by a contractor supplying entertainment on the premises of a restaurant or repairing an elevator in an office building Goldstein et al., *supra* n. 59 at 1042-1047. But the law reached into contracting within the enterprise itself.
70. In Curtis & Gartside Co. v. Pigg, 134 Pac. 1125 (Okla. 1913), a father contracted with the company for the work of his 14-year-old son. The father claimed the understanding to be that the son would not be permitted to operate dangerous machinery. The son was told by one Johnson, who was in charge of the work, to oil an unguarded saw which cut off his hand. The company agreed that such was indeed the contract; but, it maintained that it could not be liable because Johnson was a "fellow servant," and as the minor was an employee he could not sue for the negligence of a fellow servant. It was a creative argument, firmly fixed in employment law. But the Supreme Court of Oklahoma had none of it. It cut through the fellow servant rule sustaining the verdict against the company on the ground that it had "permitted or suffered" the child to do dangerous work in violation of Oklahoma's child labor law. "Suffer" means "to tolerate," the antonym of "to hinder." The language had to be given its "ordinary meaning." *Id.* at 1129.
71. United States v. Rosenwasser, 323 U.S. 360, n. 3 at 363 (1945).
72. These are set out and discussed in Labatt, *supra* n. 60, Ch. XXII(E) at pp. 2047-2068.
73. *Id.* § 749 at 2047 (italics added).

In laws enacted starting in the 1850s, arising out of a boom in railroad construction, several states made the lead company, the railroad, liable for the unpaid wages of its contractors, which the courts extended down the chain of subcontracting.[74] This judicial extension sometimes rested on a paternalistic view of those subject to the law's protection, not unlike the posture the courts had long taken toward seamen who were seen as so "reckless and improvident" as to be considered wards of the court.[75] Like seamen, these railroad construction workers were depicted by one court as "generally impoverished, degraded, ignorant and helpless" and so needful of legislative assistance.[76] The rhetoric may have been driven by the need to make a humanitarian case for exercise of the state's police power in order to overcome the legal obstacle posed by economic liberty, to the fact that the entity to be held liable was not the proximate employer. In larger perspective, however, the courts recognized that unless the law was extended up the chain of contracting, given the system of subcontracting prevalent in railroad construction, restricting the railroad's liability to the wages due employees of only the first contractor in the chain would render the wage protection a "dead letter"[77] irrespective of the moral character of the worker.

## [B] The Common Law and the Charting of Dependent Paths

The shift to an industrial economy resulted in a considerable amount of litigation in two areas where the common law was either underdeveloped or out of keeping with the times: the duration of employment; and liability for injury or loss to third parties incurred as a result of actions taken by the enterprise's workers. The resolution of each set the law on a path-dependent course that was to haunt the law a century on.

### *[1] Contract: The At-Will Rule*

English law assumed that employment was of fixed duration depending on the status of the employment: agricultural labor was hired for the year; menial or domestic servants, in absence of agreement or circumstances evidencing the contrary could be dismissed on a month's notice; the general hiring of a clerk "or other servants of a

74. *Id.* at § 785 (citing decision in Kansas, Maine, New York, Texas, Wisconsin, and Vermont).
75. Leon Fink, Sweatshops at Sea: Merchant Seamen in the World's First Globalized Industry, From 1812 to the Present 57 (2011). *See also* Matthew Rafferty, A Republic Afloat: Law, Honor, and Citizenship in Maritime America Ch. 9 (2013).
76. Mundt v. Sheboygan & Fond du Lac Rr. Co., 31 Wis. 451, 460 (1872).
77. *Id. See also* Mann v. Corrigan, 28 Kan. 194, 198 (1882); Kent v. N.Y. 628, 632 (1855); George v. Washington County Ry. Co., 44 Atl. 377, 377-378 (Me. 1899):

> Any other interpretation would nullify the statute. It is common knowledge that contracts for building railroads are nearly always taken in the first instance by construction companies or syndicates, who then let out the entire work in various divisions to subcontrators, without themselves directly employing any laborers. The most if not all the work of building the railroad is thus done by laborers directly employed by subcontractors. If these should be excluded from the statute by interpretation, its evident purpose would be defeated.

superior class" was assumed to be for a year, and so on.[78] In some cases, the periodicity of payment or the agreement for payment—so much a month or for a year—was held to state the agreed duration.[79]

In the New Republic, the assumption of fixed duration was disregarded in favor of an approach, initially, that weighed the totality of circumstances including the status of the employee, the nature of the work, the periodity of the wage or salary[80]—the latter in some jurisdictions becoming a rule.[81] By the end of the nineteenth century, however, the rule became set: that unless the circumstances of the hiring clearly evidenced an agreement for a fixed term, duration was at will.[82] In terms of legal doctrine, indefinite employment consisted of a continuous stream of moment-to-moment offers of employment by employers and acceptances of the offers by workers by the act of working. As a result, employers could change wages, hours, or other terms of employment at any moment to which the employee was deemed to assent simply by continuing to work; so, too, could the employer discharge or the employee quit without notice. To this, the Gilded Age courts added an element that was not inherent in nor bore any logical relationship to the notion of instantaneity: that the employer need not have a good reason, or any reason, or might even have a morally repugnant reason to exercise the privilege to discharge. In this way, the hiring of an employee for an indefinite term created a law-free, or lawless zone.[83]

### *[2] Tort: Responsibility for Negligence Defines Employee Status*

As with child labor, the law here has become settled. As with child labor, the settlement has had significant contemporary implications transcending the circumstances giving rise to it; but unlike the child labor solution, the path charted here has led not to potential openness but to doctrinal closure.

The growth of large industrial enterprises, especially when concentrated in areas of high population density, increased the risk that in the ordinary course of business third parties would suffer injury as a result of accidents, for example by the negligence of deliverymen. Consequently, the issue of responsibility, of liability, for those injuries became of some moment. When American courts looked to English precedent for help, as they did, they found a body of law rooted in domestic service developed in a different age; and even then, "up to the closing of years of the seventeenth century, no definite theory as to the vicarious liability of the master for the acts of his servant had

78. Ernest A. Parkyn, The Law of Master and Servant 15-17 (1897).
79. *Id.* at 17-18.
80. Labatt, *supra* n. 60, § 159 at pp. 518-519.
81. Sanford Jacoby, *The Duration of Indefinite Employment Contracts in the United States and England: An Historical Analysis*, 5 Comp. Lab. L. 85 (1982).
82. Labatt, *supra* n. 60, § 160 at pp. 516-519. As late as 1990, some courts did look to the periodicity of payment to that evidence a longer commitment. 1 H. Specter & M. Finkin, Individual Employment Law § 2.04-2.08 (1989).
83. Whence Clyde Summers, *Employment at Will in the United States: The Divine Right of Employers*, 3 U. Pa. J. Lab. & Emp. L. 65 (2000).

been formulated."[84] By the third quarter of the nineteenth century, the law became settled,[85] but not easily.[86] The difficulty lay in the lack of a persuasive rationale for the rule that eventually crystalized: that an employer was liable for the injuries to third parties caused by the negligence of its employees, when acting within the scope of their employment, but not for the negligence of its independent contractors or their employees.[87] Oliver Wendell Holmes, Jr., saw this solution as the product of an unprincipled search for the deepest pocket to bear the cost, to soak the "great corporations";[88] but, to the extent small contractors were retained by great corporations, no good reason appears to draw a line between employment and independent contractorship per se.[89]

That is, however, where the line was drawn. Because the law placed weight on the distinction between an employee and an independent contractor, the distinction became extensively litigated and drove to a set of exacting tests to distinguish the one from the other, codified in 1930 in the American Law Institute's *Restatement of Agency*.[90] The document's touchstone was the degree of control the company exercised or could exercise over the doing of the work and the worker. Situating the distinction in the law of agency is noteworthy for it underlines that it was driven by the need to allocate liability for a worker's negligence, based on little more than a hunch about who the better risk-spreader would be. As will be seen, the distinction, and so the tests giving effect to it, was to be uncoupled from its historical purpose and put to other quite unrelated use later on.

84. Labatt, *supra* n. 60 at § 2224 at 6725.
85. *Id.* at 6692-6707.
86. Note, for example, the case of Bush v. Steinman, I B&P 404 (1799) *overruled* Reedie v. London & North Wales Ry., 4 Ex. 256 (1849), in which a property owner hired a contractor to do house repairs. The contractor subcontracted part of the work. The subcontractor purchased building materials from a supplier. The supplier's worker stacked the building material on a roadside which caused a traveler's carriage to overturn. The property owner was held liable to the traveler for the negligence of the employee of the contractor's subcontractor's supplier. The decision was overruled by a half century on, but, by then, it had been cited with approval by some American courts.
87. Note the lack of doctrinal coherence. The lead company could be liable because the injury resulted from the course of the doing of its work; but, if such were the basis of the rule there would be no reason for the distinction between employees and contractors. Alternatively, imposing liability on the company could result in more careful hiring and training of employees which the company, as employer, could control but which would be more difficult to control of the employees of contractors. But, liability was available for negligent hiring, training, or supervision of employees directly. Vicarious liability added nothing on this account. As Harold Laski argued, the decision for the repose of liability was governed by policy, not doctrine. Harold Laski, *The Basis of Vicarious Liability*, 26 Yale L. J. 105, 124 (1916).
88. Oliver Wendell Holmes, Jr., *Agency II*, 5 Harv. L. Rev. 1, 14 (1891).
89. Alan Sykes, *The Economics of Vicarious Liability*, 93 Yale L.J. 1231 (1984).
90. American Law Institute, RESTATEMENT OF AGENCY § 220 (1933).

## §4.02 THE TURN AROUND: LABOR POLICY AND LAW TOWARD MID-CENTURY

Historically, employers sought three conditions in the use of labor: that it should be **stable**, **docile**, and **cheap**. Slavery bid fair to satisfy these desiderata. When free labor had to be employed, employers summoned the state to fashion law toward their ends and, in the English speaking world, at least, the state complied.[91] However, from the end of the nineteenth century into the fourth decade of the twentieth American law turned around on each of these. The law was repurposed to allow the workforce to be mobile, collectively assertive, and paid at least a politically determined minimum.

### [A] From Stability to Mobility

The provenance of the at-will rule remains without satisfactory explanation still.[92] The obvious harshness of the corollary accompanying non-duration, of legally unfettered freedom of employer action, was to become a target for reform decades later. But an effect of the at-will rule was to conduce toward the mobility of labor.[93] At the time the at-will rule was formulated and thereafter American industry experienced nearly astronomical rates of blue-collar labor turnover. Turnover reached

> 252% in a sample of Detroit factories in 1916, and the bewildering rate of 370% at Ford in 1913. The most extensive study, undertaken by the U.S. Bureau of Labor Statistics and using data from 1913-14, found a "normal" turnover rate in the factories of 115%.[94]

In South Carolina textile manufactures in 1922, fewer than 20% of the operatives lasted an entire year.[95] A 1912 study undertaken by General Electric found that the company had to hire 42, 571 persons in order to increase the payroll from 37, 237 to 42, 971; that is, six and a third times as many people had to be hired as constituted the permanent increase.[96]

---

91. Masters, Servants, and Magistrates in Britain & the Empire, 1562-1955 (Douglas Hay & Paul Craven, eds. 2004); Christopher Tomlins, Freedom Bound: Law, Labor, and Civic Identity in Colonizing English America, 1580-1965 (2010). Southern textile mills used their control of village schools toward this indoctrinal end: "[I]t was believed that education tended to increase the strength of management authority. A docile, pliable worker was more easily controlled and supervised." Cathy McHugh, Mill Family: The Labor System in the Southern Cotton Textile Industry 1880-1915, 64 (1988).
92. The various theories are laid out and critiqued by Andrew Morriss, *Exploding Myths: An Empirical and Economic Reassessment of the Rise of Employment At-Will*, 59 Mo. L. Rev. 679 (1994). Alas, Morriss' own theory fares no better. *See* the text accompanying n. 260, *infra*.
93. Were the employment to be held of, say, a month's duration, the employee would have been legally obligated to give a month's notice in order to quit and would be potentially liable in damages for quitting upon giving less notice, or none.
94. Daniel Rodgers, The Work Ethics in Industrial America, 1850-1920, 163 (1978) (references omitted).
95. D. Carlton, Mill and Town in South Carolina, 1880-1920, 151-52 (1982).
96. Ronald Schatz, The Electrical Workers 17 (1983).

Two other features on the legal scene should be noted in that connection: one, wage payment law, which requires some exploration; the other, the fallout from the Thirteenth Amendment's abolition of involuntary servitude, which requires little.

### *[1] Wage Payment*

One of the contests between the market and the law in the Gilded Age involved efforts by reformers to have the American states enact a domestic version of the English Truck Act of 1831. These were sought as a consequence of the practice of employees in remote locations, particularly in mining and textile manufacture, where the employers owned the only residential and commercial facilities available for the workforce, to pay employees in company scrip redeemable only in the company's store, which charged inflated prices,[97] or by similar devices. The legislative response was to require payment in U.S. currency at regular, relatively short intervals with all wages earned to be paid out on the termination of employment.[98] The U.S. Supreme Court sustained Tennessee's law, applied to forbid a coal mine to pay miners in bushels of coal, on the ground that, as the Tennessee court put it, the law placed "the employer and employee upon equal ground in the matter of wages."[99] In other words, the law saw the employee as labor market participant and sought to redress the imbalance in bargaining power.

But these laws did more. Payment in scrip effectively bound the worker to be in a place where the scrip could be redeemed and so bound the worker to the employer. The worker could break free only with difficulty.[100] By requiring the timely payment of all wages earned in U.S. currency these laws implicitly, and sometimes expressly, legislated against the common practice of withholding wages as a bond for the employee's giving timely notice of leaving employment.[101] As quitting before the notice

97. A study of coal mining in West Virginia in the early twentieth century observed that,

> in remote locations, company store prices ranged from 5 to 12% more than they were in towns where independent stores existed nearby. [Mine owner W.P.] Tams recalled that his fellow operators "charged all the market would bear" so that profits on their merchandise would offset losses they often suffered when coal prices fell.

James Green, The Devil Is Here in These Hills 22 (2015) (reference omitted).

98. Robert Patterson, Wage Payment Legislation in the United States (1918).
99. Harbison v. Knoxville Iron Co., 53 SW 955, 960 (Tenn. 1899) *aff'd* Knoxville Iron Co. v. Harbison, 183 U.S. 13 (1901).
100. Currarino, *supra* n. 34 at 97.
101. The U.S. Supreme Court sustained the constitutionality of just such a law: it provided that on the discharge of any employee, with or without cause, by any company engaged in railroading or railroad construction,

> the unpaid wages of any such servant or employee, then earned at the contract rate, *without abatement or deduction*, shall be, and become due and payable on the day of such discharge, or refusal to longer employ … .

St. Louis, Iron Mountain and St. Paul Ry Co. v. Paul, 173 U.S. 404, 405 (1899) (italics added). A few states allowed forfeitures for quitting without due notice, but only if the employer was equally bound to give notice of termination. The laws are set out in Labatt, *supra* n. 60 §§ 874,

period had been exhausted would result, in effect, in a forfeiture of accrued wages,[102] the device was intended to hoard trained labor. The eradication of payment in scrip and compelled wage withholding bolstered the power of workers as market participants, as persons who could quit, or threaten to quit, at any time without fear of immediate economic loss. Additionally, wage payment law resolved for practical purposes what had been a hotly debated issue and a sharp doctrinal divide in the law of employment contracts.

In the early nineteenth century when labor, most often agricultural, was hired for a year or was otherwise hired for stated term the courts adhered to the British rule: that as the contract was "entire," an employee who performs only part of it and then ceases to perform the remainder without good cause was held to have abandoned the employment and had no right to be compensated for the work already done.[103] The rule seemed harsh even at the time, and a minority of jurisdictions sought ways around it, most famously by the Supreme Court of New Hampshire's 1834 decision in *Britton* v. *Turner*[104] which held an action in *quantum meruit*, for the value of the services performed, could be brought. The court stressed the illogic and practical harshness of the entire contract rule,[105] but it made no comment on what would seem to be the policy behind it: by working on pain of total loss should the worker find a better job, the rule gave the employer the upper hand on assuring the stability of the workforce.

Some jurisdictions also sought to ameliorate the asperity of the entire contract rule by looking to the periodicity of payment rather than to the contract's total duration to find the contract to be divisible, not entire.[106] This allowed for only some recovery, and, as Carl McGowan pointed out in 1935, the approach suffered on that account. But, as he noted, by that time the issue had been largely rendered moot: wage payment laws, by requiring the payment of all wages due in regular and relatively short intervals

---

875 at pp. 2319-2322 (Maine, Massachusetts, New Jersey, Pennsylvania, Rhode Island, Wisconsin).

102. Some states, Tennessee is one, disallowed forfeiture. Schimpf v. Tennessee Mfg. Co., 6 S.W. 131 (Tenn. 1887). But, where the provision was recast as a liquidated damage, because the damage to the company from the loss of services was incalculable, in this case, of a minor in a cotton mill—the court conjured up the possibility of the mill's having to shut down because the minor had quit, though it had not and, in fact, the minor had offered to return to work—the provision was enforced. *See, e.g.*, Tennessee Mfg. Co. v. James, 18 S.W. 262 (Tenn. 1892).

103. Labatt, *supra* n. 60 §§ 491-492.

104. 6 N.H. 481 (1834). Labatt, *supra* n. 60 §§ 501-502.

105. Britton v. Turner, *id.* at 486-487:

> A party who contracts to perform certain specified labor, and who breaks his contract in the first instance, without any attempt to perform it, can only be made liable to pay the damages which the other party has sustained by reason of such non performance, which in many instances may be trifling—whereas a party who in good faith has entered upon the performance of his contract, and nearly completed it, and then abandoned the further performance—although the other party has had the full benefit of all that has been done, and has purhaps sustained no actual damage—is in fact subjected to a loss of all which has been performed, in the nature of damages for the non fulfilment of the remainder, upon the technical rule, that the contract must be fully performed in order to a recovery of any part of the compensation.

106. Labatt *supra* n. 60 at §503.

and of all due on quitting/discharge "inexorably clamp divisibility down on large classes of employment contracts."[107] With the mobility-suppressing advantage of the entire contract rule thus extinguished, employers could enjoy the freedom the at-will rule gave them, the mobility-enhancing consequences of that rule adding nothing for workers beyond what wage payment law did.

### *[2] Debt Bondage*

In order to hold workers to their work contracts, especially for work in remote and harsh locations, for example in Maine's logging camps, a number of states made the quitting of work a crime. The means they used were legally artful, ostensibly grounded in fraud which had long been subject to criminal sanction. These laws turned on an advance having being given the worker, in money or transportation, the worker's acceptance without intent to perform, and the worker's subsequent nonperformance—quitting—which the law made prima facie evidence of intent not to perform at the time the advance was given.[108] The U.S. Immigration Commission studied these laws in 1908 and found that they produced a system of peonage.[109] Of the Commission's fieldwork in Maine, the Commission observed,

> The contract-labor law has become a club which the foremen and superintendents draw upon the laborers who refuse to go to work or to continue at work. If a man leaves his employer before settling for advances, he will be pursued and apprehended, or someone will telephone to the constable, who will arrest the laborer. He will then be brought before the justice, and "sent down the river," to prison; or if he consents to labor until he shall have reimbursed for all advances and the fine and cost of the prosecution, the employer will settle with the court and constable and will take the laborer back into the forest. No doubt many of the laborers never attempt to escape, although they may consider that they have been basely deceived about the conditions of labor.[110]

Alabama's law was one of the more Draconian. Not only did it make the quit prima facie evidence of fraud, Alabama's law of evidence also disallowed a defendant to testify to his uncommunicated intentions.

In 1911, the U.S. Supreme Court cut through the artifice:

> We cannot escape the conclusion that, although the statute in terms is to punish fraud, still its natural and inevitable effect is to expose to conviction for crime those who simply fail or refuse to perform contracts for personal service in liquidation of a debt, and judging its purpose by its effect that it seeks in this way to provide the means of compulsion through which performance of such service may be secured. The question is whether such a statute is constitutional.[111]

107. Carl McGowan, *The Divisibility of Employment Contracts*, 21 Iowa L. Rev. 50, 67 (1935).
108. Labatt *supra* n. 60 at §320.
109. II Reports of United States Immigration Commission, *Peonage* at 443-449 (1911).
110. *Id.* at 449.
111. Bailey v. Alabama, 219 U.S. 219, 238 (1911).

The answer was that it was not: By creating a state of peonage—debt bondage—the law violated the Thirteenth Amendment's prohibition of involuntary servitude. In 1944, the Court made it clear that the evil in the law was not that quitting was made a prima facie evidence of intent to defraud, nor the lack of testimonial capacity of the worker to address her intent. Simply put, "no state can make the quitting of work any component of a crime" —that the policy of the federal Antipeonage Act, enforcing the Thirteenth Amendment, was to "maintain a system of completely free and voluntary labor throughout the United States."[112]

The Court emphasized that the evil of peonage was neither sectional nor racial.[113] At the century's turn, however, a number of southern states had enacted anti-enticement laws making it a crime to offer or give employment to a "servant" whom the employer knows to be under contract to work for another for stated duration, most often contracts of tenancy and sharecropping, sometimes explicitly and exclusively so.[114] These *were* sectional and, in practice, race-based. As the Supreme Court of Georgia observed, these laws were enacted to prevent "the derangement of an entire system of labor,"[115] that is, to adjust to the abolition of slavery. As the worker could not be held in debt bondage, these laws enforced labor stability by regulating putative employers. The laws were fraught with legal issues—who was a "servant" made subject to it, whether the law applied to an offer made before the worker commenced to work, or to a worker who had already, if wrongfully, quit, and more—but, they did not apply to offers made to workers who were at-will and so free to quit. Consequently, they became dead letters with eclipse of sharecropping and the dominance of at-will labor.

These anti-enticement laws resonated against and added the force of criminal sanction to the tort of intentional interference with an existing economic advantage. An employer is free to entice an at-will employee by an offer of better terms. Any idea to the contrary—that, for example, an employer so enjoyed the "goodwill" his worker generated that the employee's leaving to accept a better job could be actionable—was essayed and found untenable.[116] But, now as then, an offer of a better job to induce one who is known to the offeror to be bound for a term—or to be bound by a covenant not to compete—could, if accepted, be actionable in tort.[117] Covenants not to compete and other obstacles to mobility on the contemporary scene will be taken up below.

112. Pollock v. Williams, 322 U.S. 4, 18 (1944).
113. *Id.* at 11.
114. Labatt, *supra* n. 60 at §§ 2614-2627.
115. Bryan v. State, 44 Ga. 328, 332 (1871).
116. As Learned Hand put it, "The result of the contrary would be intolerable, both to such employers as could use the employé more effectively and to such employés as might receive added pay. It would put an end to any kind of competition." Triangle Film Corp. v. Artcraft Pictures Corp., 250 Fed. 981, 982 (2nd Cir. 1918).
117. 2 Howard Specter & Matthew Finkin, Individual Employment Law and Litigation § 13.07 (1989) (cases cited in nn. 58-59 at p. 109).

## [B] From Docility to Collective Assertiveness

### *[1] The Norris-LaGuardia Act*

After nightfall in the fall of 1901 organized labor's most famous heroine—or infamous agitator—Mary Harris "Mother" Jones—addressed forty miners assembled surreptitiously on a mountain slope above the Kellys Creek Coal Mining Company's mine and the company-owned town where the miners lived. She exhorted them to be men, not "cringing serfs," and to join the United Mine Workers of America, founded a decade earlier. They all took the "oath of obligation" joining the union; but they were observed and reported on by company spies. When they reported for work in the morning they were fired, told to evacuate their company's houses, and told they would never work in the valley again—that they were being blacklisted.[118] The company's actions were altogether lawful, though blacklisting workers for their union activity or sympathies, a practice that had become common in railroading and mining, had by that time been legislated against in a number of states of which, however, West Virginia was not one.[119]

Coal mining in southwestern West Virginia was typical of the intense anti-unionism espoused by American employers at the time, though it took a particularly virulent and violent form there. About two decades later, on May 8, 1920, the Red Jacket Consolidated Coal and Coke Company announced that it would not employ any union members. Years later, a Red Jacket miner reflected on the day he joined the union: "I took the obligation on a Saturday," he recalled, "and we was thrown out on Monday. They told us we'd have to get out or sign the yaller dog, one-or-t' other."[120]

The "yellow dog" was labor parlance for contracts employees were required to sign whereby they eschewed union membership or support and often a variety of other means whereby they might join together to make common cause. The term was applied, for example, to leases that coal miners had to sign for company housing. The U.S. Coal Commission's investigation into the restriction of the civil liberties of coal miners in West Virginia in the 1920s found these leases particularly odious. It singled out one for illustration and denunciation. It read thusly:

> The lessee hereby further agrees not to use, allow, *suffer, or permit* the use of said premises, or the private ways or roads through and over other lands of the lessor used to reach said premises from the public road, for any purpose other than going in to said premises from the public road, and out from the same to said public road, by himself and the members of his family; and, further, to do no act or thing, nor suffer or cause the same to be done, whereby the public or any person or persons whomsoever may be invited or allowed to go or trespass upon said premises, or upon said private ways or roads, or upon other grounds of the lessor, except

118. The episode is recounted by James Green, The Devil Is Here in These Hills: West Virginia's Coal Miners and Their Battle for Freedom 43-44 (2015).
119. Labatt, *supra* n. 60 at § 2031. Allowing himself the privilege of editorial comment, which he rarely exercised. Labatt termed the practice of blacklisting "essentially repugnant to the free institutions of Anglo-Saxon civilization."
120. Green, *supra* n. 118 at 203.

> physicians attending the lessee and his family; teamsters or draymen moving lessee and his family belonging into said premises or away from the same; and undertakers with hearse, carriages and drivers, and friends, in case of death of the lessee or any member of his family.[121]

The prohibition on any visitor entering the home—other than those moving household furnishings in or out, doctors attending to an ill miner or morticians taking them out—was meant to make it difficult for union organizers, or even co-workers, to discuss common grievances and the possibility of collective resistance.

The yellow dog assumed a significant legal role by virtue of the U.S. Supreme Court's decision in the *Hitchman Coal* case in 1917.[122] Inasmuch as employees served on an at-will basis and could be discharged for joining a union, the Yellow Dog Contract had no legal effect on the employer's ability to discharge a worker for union activity. But, because the Court sustained its lawfulness, efforts by unions to organize the workers with knowledge that they were contractually bound not to do so would be an effort to induce a breach of contract and could be subject to injunction. Employers were quick to seize on this device resulting in sweeping injunctions against union organizing efforts—one involving the Red Jacket mine so sweeping and so odious that the nomination of Judge John J. Parker to the U.S. Supreme Court failed because he had approved it. More than that, "An almost endless array of legal games were played by employers that made almost all collective action by workers susceptible to legal prohibitions."[123] Joel Seidman's 1932 doctoral dissertation, *The Yellow Dog Contract*, catalogued many of these: promises to "adjust all differences by means of individual bargaining"[124] at the Exchange Bakery and Restaurant in New York City; to renounce any "concerted action [with co-workers] with a view to securing greater compensation," as at the Moline Plow Company in Moline, Illinois[125]; or to "arbitrate all differences" according to the machinery set up by the employer and its company union at the United Railways & Electric Company of Baltimore.[126] So, too, did a contemporary compilation by Elliot Cohen who provided a nuanced taxonomy of yellow dog contracts.[127]

Organized labor had sought federal legislation against the labor injunction since 1906 and, after the *Hitchman* case, against the yellow dog. In 1927, a progressive group in the U.S. Senate introduced a law drafted by a private drafting group that included Felix Frankfurter, later to be appointed to the U.S. Supreme Court, and Edwin Witte, who was later to write the Social Security Act. The law was sponsored in the Senate by

121. U.S. Coal Comm'n, Report of the United States Coal Commission, S. Doc. No. 68-195, pt. 1, at 169 (1925) (emphasis added). The Common found these to be "obnoxious and inconsistent with the spirit of free local communities." *Id.* at 169-70. I have emphasized the lawyer's artful borrowing of the phrase "suffer or permit" used to protect child labor to repress the workers' ability to engage in social intercourse.
122. Hitchman Coal & Coke Co. v. Mitchell, 245 U.S. 229 (1917).
123. Daniel Jacoby, Laboring for Freedom: A New Look at the History of Labor in America 62 (1998).
124. Joel Seidman, The Yellow Dog Contract 58 (1932).
125. *Id.* at 66.
126. *Id.* at 69.
127. Elliot Cohen, The Yellow Dog Contract (1932).

George Norris and in the House by Fiorello LaGuardia. The measure failed in 1927, but it was passed into law on the heels of a political shift in 1932 as the Norris–LaGuardia Act.

The key features of the Act will be discussed momentarily, but it is imperative to stress that it was advocated on grounds of civil liberty: that in labor disputes, broadly defined, employees could not be forbidden to come to the aid of others nor forbidden to enlist others in aid of themselves. The evil of the Yellow Dog Contract that advocates for its extirpation condemned was the atomization of those made subject to it. One illustration will stand for all. Senator Norris, who had visited the miners in southwestern West Virginia, pointed to the plight of the laboring man:

> His family can not have food to eat or clothes to wear unless he gets a job. If he gets a job, he must surrender his liberty ... . He can not associate with his fellows. In connection with his fellows, he can not present a grievance to the employer. He has agreed to make no such demand ... . *He must singly present any grievance he has.* He must abide by the decision which is thus given him. He has no appeal. *He has no opportunity to join with his fellows and make his demands effective.* In effect, if he must live and support his family and clothes his children, he must surrender his liberty.[128]

The Norris–LaGuardia Act denied the federal courts the power to issue injunctions in most labor disputes, defined to include individual controversies as well as collective controversies. But it did more. Section 2 declared it to be the "public policy" of the U.S. that the individual worker "shall be free from the interference, restraint, or coercion of employers of labor, or their agents, in the designation of such representatives or in self-organization or in ... **concerted activities** for the purpose of collective bargaining **or other mutual aid or protection**."[129] Section 3 provided that,

> **Any undertaking or promise** ... in conflict with the public policy declared in section 2 of this Act, is hereby declared to be contrary to the public policy of the United States, shall not be enforceable in any court of the United States and shall not afford any basis for the granting of legal or equitable relief by any such court.[130]

Section 4 went on to particularize concerted acts for mutual aid or protection that the Act shielded from judicial prohibition, that nailed down the reach of the general clause in those situations. And section 15 repealed all laws or any part of any extant law that conflicted with the Act. It is difficult to conceive that a law so purposed could have been more tightly crafted nor more emphatic.

Because the reach of federal power over employment under the Interstate Commerce clause was extremely narrow at the time, the Norris–LaGuardia approached the subject of employee liberty from the standpoint of that which Congress could control—the power of the federal courts. Employers were not constrained in their ability to impose yellow dog restrictions; but, the federal courts could not enforce them. Congress turned to what employers could not do three years later.

---

128. 75 Cong. Rec. 4504 (1932) (remarks of Sen. Norris) (emphasis added).
129. 29 U.S.C. §2 (emphasis added).
130. *Id.* §3 (emphasis added).

### *[2] The National Labor Relations Act*

To set the stage: to some, the overarching question raised by the Great Depression was whether capitalism was coming to an end; but to others, less dire diagnoses for the Depression were essayed. Some saw "predatory" or "destructive" competition that cut prices and drove down wages—that reduced workers' purchasing power—to be the culprit. Others, harkening back to the 1880s, and echoing explanations offered for the Panics of 1873 and 1893,[131] saw the displacement of labor by machine production, which took on the antiseptic sobriquet of "technological unemployment,"[132] to be the perpetrator.

Congress responded initially in the National Industrial Recovery Act (NIRA) of 1933. It would cartelize business—in which cartels organized labor could participate—and allow these cartels to promulgate codes having the force of law governing prices and wages. This, it was thought, would eliminate cutthroat competition, raise wages, and increase consumption. The NIRA was held unconstitutional.

Even before the dust had settled on the constitutional status of the NIRA, Senator Robert F. Wagner had set about to address afresh what had long been seen as the quintessential labor question, not only of securing higher wages and better hours and working conditions, but overarching that: "how to reconcile the democratic promise of the nation with the profoundly undemocratic organization of industry."[133] How could a waged worker be a citizen, an autonomous participant in the political sphere, while inured to a pervasive system of plenary managerial control at work, and in life away from work as well,[134] in all of which the worker had no say? "Must this not mean," wrote Louis Brandeis,

---

131. Meg Jacobs, Pocketbook Politics: Economic Citizenship in Twentieth Century America 146 (2005). *See also* text accompanying *supra* nn. 32 & 33.

132. As Sanford Jacoby explains, "The term 'technological unemployment' was coined in the 1920s, when elastic credit and a pent-up demand for plant and equipment helped to fuel a mechanization boom that resulted in the displacement of large numbers of workers." Sanford Jacoby, Employing Bureaucracy 168 (1985). A Brookings Institute study of the National Industrial Recovery Act felt it necessary to take the issue up:

> A realization of the fact that the introduction of machines causes at least temporary unemployment is at least as old as the Industrial Revolution; but the rapid technology advance of recent years, striking instances of displacement of men by machinery, and the advancing "rationalization" of American industry between 1922 and 1929 had given the idea of technological unemployment a new interest and had made large numbers of persons susceptible to proposals which seemed to show a way toward spreading the available work.

Leverett Lyon et al., The National Recovery Administration: An Analysis and Appraisal 6 (1935). The debate among economists is traced by Gregory Woirol, The Technological Unemployment and Structural Unemployment Debates Chs. 4 & 5 (1996). I am indebted to Professor Jacoby for bringing this resource to my attention.

133. White, *supra* n. 1 at 74. *See also* Washington Gladden, The Labor Question 99 (1911) ("So shall we realize our democracy. It has never been anything more than the skeleton of a democracy; so long as industry in feudalistic it cannot be.").

134. The New England mills imposed strict moral codes on the young girls who worked in them, which is understandable as the mills stood in the shoes of the girls' parents. David A.

> that the American who is brought up with the idea of political liberty must surrender what every citizen deems far more important, his industrial liberty? Can this contradiction—our general political liberty and this industrial slavery—long coexist? Either political liberty will be extinguished or industrial liberty must be restored.[135]

The concern was widely shared in reform circles.[136]

In 1919, Woodrow Wilson called for legislation "based upon a full recognition of the right of those who work ... to participate in some organic way in every decision which directly affects their welfare or the part they are to play in industry."[137] It would take more than a decade, of yet more strife and violence and a depression so deep as to dissipate public confidence in business before Congress would enact a law, the National Labor Relations Act (Labor Act).

Five features of the law bear mention here for the law's relevance into the twenty-first century. First, it extended a federal right to statutory employees to engage in collective bargaining by a representative of *their* choosing—rendering company-sponsored representation systems unlawful—but only if a majority of employees in a governmentally defined "bargaining unit" has chosen to be represented. That is, the law was built on the regnant model of mass production industries, on an assumption of stable complements of workers who would comprise "bargaining units" for which a

---

Zonderman, ASPIRATIONS AND ANXIETIES: NEW ENGLAND WORKERS AND THE MECHANIZED FACTORY SYSTEM 1815-1850, 150 (1992). But control of private life was not restricted to child labor. Southern textile mills in the 1920s policed their workers' habits and domestic life. Jacquelyn Dowd Hall et al., LIKE A FAMILY: THE MAKING OF A SOUTHERN COTTON MILL WORLD 123-26 (1987). Corporate welfare plans often involved intrusive systems of oversight and control. Stuart Brandes, AMERICAN WELFARE CAPITALISM, 1880-1940, 138-30 (1976). The assertion of the right of management to control their workers' private lives continues unabated. Robert Howie & Laurence Shapiro, *Lifestyle Discrimination Statutes: A Dangerous Erosion of At-Will Employment, a Passing Fad, or Both?*, 31 Emp. Rel. L.J. 21 (2005). The latter's argument jibes nicely with Clyde Summers' critique of plenary management control claimed as if by Divine Right. Summers, *supra* n. 83. The trope is not hyperbolic. In 1902 George Baer, spokesman for the anthracite coal operators confronting a miners' strike, replied to a correspondent who'd urged conciliation, thusly:

> The rights and interests of the laboring man will be protected and cared for—not by the labor agitators, but by the Christian men to whom God in his infinite wisdom has given the control of the property interests of the country ... .

*Quoted in* Witt Bowen, THE INDUSTRIAL HISTORY OF THE UNITED STATES 390 (1930).

135. Louis Brandeis, THE CURSE OF BIGNESS 39 (1934).

136. *See, e.g.*, Donald Richberg, THE RAINBOW 47 (1936) ("To put it bluntly, an economic autocracy and a democratic government cannot support each other long. There will be an eventual choice between the ideals of mastery and service."). Richberg was a Chicago lawyer who represented railroad unions and played a role in drafting federal labor legislation. A. Lincoln Filene, A MERCHANT'S HORIZON 47 (1924) ("And it is still harder to see how we can much longer send Jones the worker in steel or shoes or sealing-wax to the exercise of his rights as an American, and if an industrial order in which he is habituated to an autocratic control that was old before his country was born."). Filene owned a major department store in Boston and was active in reform efforts. In the debate on the Norris-LaGuardia Act, Senator Wagner argued: "If into this condition of affairs [the accumulation of capital] we should inject the archaic notion of master and servant, what kind of citizenship will inhabit the continent in the next generation?" 75 Cong. Rec. 4918 (1932).

137. 58 Cong. Rec. 40, 41 (1919).

franchise could be exercised for representation. (In 1959, the law was amended to facilitate representation in a segment of work performed on a casual basis, in the construction trades; but only for those workers.) Second, if a representative is selected, it would become the exclusive representative of all the workers in the unit. No provision was made for representation of only those who have joined the union. Third, because of federal supremacy, any state law that infringed upon the zone of federal regulation—not only laws that would make lawful that which federal law prohibits, but those that prohibit that which federal law also prohibits—were swept away *sub silentio* (for the law did not address this issue) by operation of the constitution's provision making federal law supreme. Fourth, the law's prohibitions were placed in the hands of a federal administrative agency which, for administrative reasons, was denied the power to order full compensation for victims of employer retaliation or to impose contract terms. That is, the law depended as much if not more for its realization on voluntary compliance—effected by the exercise of employee self-help, the strike—then on legal coercion. And last, though the law is principally concerned with collective bargaining it included the right set out in the Norris-LaGuardia Act to engage in "other concerted activity for mutual aid or protection" outside of collective bargaining or union representation.

To anticipate subsequent discussion it pays to note here the purchase that that provision has, borrowing from the idea of workers' civil liberties which played so prominent a role in the debate on the Norris-LaGuardia Act whence that provision was taken. When a union sought to circulate literature in the workplace in support of an increase in the minimum wage and the employer forbade it on the ground that the employer had no control in the matter—that as it was a political subject and as the workplace was not a political forum the union had no right to put the employer's property to that use—the U.S. Supreme Court rejected the employer's argument. The right to engage in concerted activity for mutual aid or protection encompasses the resort to channels outside the workplace and on fronts other than collective bargaining. Employees had the right "to improve working conditions through [collective] resort to administrative and judicial forums" and by appeals to the legislature free of employer restraint or interference.[138]

Note that the case arose under the Labor Act's protection of employees against any restraint by employees of their right to engage in concerted activity for mutual protection, not collective bargaining. The fact that a union was circulating the petition satisfied the requirement of concert of action, but that has long been understood to require no more than the minimum of a speaker and listener. The legal result would not change a bit were a group of workers in a nonunionized workplace to have circulated the same petition: it would be concerted activity for their mutual aid or protection which the employer could not forbid.

To return to the history, in 1947, a Republican Congress enacted the Taft-Hartley Act over President Truman's veto, cutting back on the Labor Act's encouragement of collective bargaining. Taft-Hartley was intended to blunt union organizing and to

138. Eastex, Inc. v. NLRB, 437 U.S. 556, 565 (1978).

weaken union bargaining power,[139] which, over time, it did. Of special interest here, however, is Congress' rejection in 1947 of the Labor Act's test of economic dependence to determine those eligible to engage in collective bargaining. Taft–Hartley restricted the definition of a statutory employee to the common law's agency test fashioned to determine vicarious liability for negligence. That decision would have significant consequences in the next century.

Despite the longer-term blunting effects of the 1947 amendments, the Labor Act's answer to The Labor Question was responsive for more than a generation. Union density in the private sector grew: by mid-century, one out of every three American workers was represented by a union, predominately in large mass production industries. Collective bargaining reduced wage inequality and placed an upward pressure on wages that rippled outside the unionized sector.[140] The exercise of independent voice within the enterprise lessened arbitrary treatment and drove toward greater workplace fairness.[141]

### [C] From Cheap Labor to a Minimum Wage

The Fair Labor Standards Act of 1938 was one of the most difficult pieces of New Deal legislation: opposition, on constitutional, economic, and sectional grounds, was intense. President Roosevelt had to try three times to get a wage and hour law enacted, watering the bill down each time.[142] The policy the law states is to secure "the minimum standard of living necessary for health, efficiency, and general well-being of workers";[143] but, the emphasis of later development has, in practice, been *sub silentio* on the qualification "minimum," which emphasis, however, was instinct in the argument for measure. Carroll Daugherty's 1935 study, *Labor Problems in American Industry*, pointed to the connection between low wages and malnutrition, with further effect on the prevalence of illness and stunted child development.[144] In the final effort to get the law through, President Roosevelt pointed to workers having pay "so low they ... suffer great hardship, they are unable to buy adequate food and shelter ... [or] to maintain health."[145] He put the law to Congress this way: no

> reasonable person seek[s] an immediate and drastic change from the lowest pay to the highest pay. We are seeking, of course, only legislation *to end starvation wages* and intolerable hours; more desirable wages are and should continue to be the product of collective bargaining.[146]

139. Howell Harris, The Right to Manage: Industrial Relations Policies of American Business in the 1940s, 125-127 (1982).
140. Derek Bok & John Dunlop, Labor and the American Community 287-289 (1970).
141. *Id.* at 465. ("Unions ... have made enormous strides to eliminate error, malice, favoritism, and other human failings in the dismissal, discipline, promotion, and preferment of employees.")
142. J. Grossman, *Fair Labor Standards Act of 1938: Maximum Struggle for a Minimum Wage*, 101 Monthly Labor Rev. 22 (1978).
143. 20 U.S.C. § 202(a).
144. Carroll Daugherty, Labor Problems in American Industry 207-08 (1933).
145. Annual Message to the Congress (Jan. 3, 1938) *in* F.D. Roosevelt, Papers and Addresses 5 (1941).
146. *Id.* at 6 (emphasis added). The latter was a concession—or sop—to the American Federation of Labor which opposed the minimum wage on the ground that wages should be set by collective bargaining and that a legislated minimum would become the de facto maximum.

The motive force, as the Senate report on the measure put it, was to raise employees above the danger of "wages too low to buy the bare necessities of life."[147] Illustration 2 is a 1939 comment on the then recently enacted the Fair Labor Standards Act (FLSA). Note how the depiction echoes President Franklin Roosevelt's characterization of the law as a bulwark against starvation.

**Illustration 2**

Reprinted with the permission of the State Historical Society of Missouri, Fitzpatrick Cartoon Collection.

147. Sen. Rep. No. 884 (75th Cong., 1st sess.) *cited* in U.S. v. Rosenwasser, 323 U.S. 360, 361 (1945).

Two other aspects New Deal legislation bear mention here. First, the FLSA required a 50% wage premium on overtime work in an effort to encourage hiring instead of assigning overtime hours to incumbent workers. The "time and a half" rule for overtime applied to all nonexempt workers, not only those working at the minimum wage. Consequently, that provision has more practical meaning for most employees today than does the minimum wage.

Second, the intermittency of work, which had been a subject of concern before the Depression,[148] was now addressed. The Social Security Act of 1935 provided for a federally sponsored, state enacted and administered system of unemployment compensation.[149]

These measures—wage, hour, and unemployment compensation law—wove the institution of waged work more tightly into the social fabric. Work would be paid at a level that was at least politically acceptable. Periods of work loss due to no fault of the worker's would be smoothed out: the qualifying workers would, in effect, be paid to look for work in a society in which job holding had become an earmark of citizenship.

## §4.03 TOWARD THE CENTURY'S END

The ensuing decades after the Second World War witnessed the consolidation and extension of the model of the large[150] vertically integrated corporation. Indeed, there was a movement in the sixties toward the conglomerization of enterprises that shared no common product or service at all.[151]

As the century progressed, Congress expanded and bolstered economic citizenship through antidiscrimination in employment laws, and, to the same effect, cabined the exercise of managerial prerogative under the at-will rule when workers were dismissed in contravention of a statutorily stated public purpose. Congress continued

148. Sumner Slichter, THE TURNOVER OF FACTORY LABOR (1919); Paul Brissenden & Emily Frankel, LABOR TURNOVER IN INDUSTRY: A STATISTICAL ANALYSIS (1922).
149. The political and social history is explored by Daniel Rogers, UNEMPLOYMENT INSURANCE: THE AMERICAN EXPERIENCE, 1915-1935 (1969).
150. Note three rather different businesses in the period 1935-1960: Kodak, whose key product was photographic film; Sears Roebuck, the nation's largest mail-order retailer; and Thompson Products, a manufacturer of precision engine parts.

*Number of Employees*

| | *Kodak* | *Sears Roebuck* | *Thompson Products* |
|---|---|---|---|
| 1935 | 17,840 | 49,500 | 2,150 |
| 1960 | 45,860 | 207,000 | 22,970 |

*Source*: Sanford Jacoby, Modern Manors: Welfare Capitalism Since the New Deal Table 2.1 at p. 38 (1997).

151. However, the Taft-Hartley Act's prohibition of the secondary boycott was successful in limiting the ability of unions to extend economic pressure upward to the owning enterprise. Robert Gorman & Matthew Finkin, LABOR LAW: ANALYSIS AND ADVOCACY § 12.4 ("The Ally Doctrine: Common Ownership and Control") (2013).

to ameliorate specific asperities of wage labor: attending to workplace safety and health, although with questionable practical impact[152]; partially to protect the security of guaranteed benefits pension systems[153]; to require abbreviated notice of plant closings or mass layoffs[154]; to begin to acknowledge that technology could be invasive of worker privacy[155]; to begin to address the conflict between the demands of work and family by providing for a limited period of unpaid family leave.[156]

The states continued to legislate on emerging issues, performing their traditional role of legal experiment stations. In contrast, the state courts took one step forward in contract, then took one step back; and a half-step forward in tort. These are outlined below.

## [A] Legislation

### *[1] Employment Discrimination and Economic Citizenship*

If the answer to The Labor Question was to be found in "economic citizenship," in labor market participation, by mid-century America had to grapple with the exclusion or restriction of significant groups from the market. The status of women was an issue even in antebellum times: the role of women as workers was commonly thought discordant with their role as wives and mothers, which conflict was exacerbated as more women entered the world of waged work.[157] The integration of black workers after Reconstruction was fraught with what was, to many white workers, unacceptable consequences insofar as it implied "social equality."[158] To this, the hostility of American workers to specific ethnic groups, usually first or second generation

152. The Occupational Safety and Health Act of 1970, 29 U.S.C. § 651 et seq.
153. The Employee Retirement Income Security Act of 1974, 29 U.S.C. § 1001 et seq.
154. The Worker Adjustment and Retraining Notification Act of 1988, 29 U.S.C. § 2101 et seq.
155. Employee Polygraph Protection Act of 1988, 29 U.S.C. § 2001 et seq.
156. The Family and Medical Leave Act of 1993, 29 U.S.C. § 2601 et seq.
157. Alice Kessler-Harris, OUT TO WORK: A HISTORY OF WAGE EARNING WOMEN IN THE UNITED STATES (1982).
158. The animosity of some white union members to the admission of blacks was quite vocal. Sterling Spero & Abram Harris, THE BLACK WORKER: A STUDY OF THE NEGRO AND THE LABOR MOVEMENT (1931). In response to an effort to admit blacks to the Brotherhood of Railway Carmen in 1921, one delegate's comments were reported thusly:

> "I do not think," he said, "there is a member in this room that believes in taking the Negro in with him on social equality. I believe that God in his infinite mercy made the Negro but he never made him to be a car worker. I do not believe the time will ever come when he should come into a union along with carmen … . I want to tell you that I am a northern man … . I was born with an abolitionist father; but when the time does come that I must sit down in social equality with the Negro … . I want to be carried to the nearest insane asylum."

*Id.* at 66. *See also* Ray Marshall, THE NEGRO WORKER (1967). The attitude of the southern railroad unions representing the "running trades" toward black workers has been attributed to economic as well as social concerns. Paul Taillon, GOOD, RELIABLE, WHITE MEN: RAILROAD BROTHERHOODS, 1877-1917, 154-155 (2009). In contrast, James Green documents the fact that black and immigrant Italian miners were often the most militant union members in the West Virginia coal fields and the United Mine Workers insisted on the complete equality of its

immigrants who competed with them for jobs has to be added, especially the Chinese.[159] Hostility so grounded had a long pedigree. In 1850, an effort was mounted in California to prohibit Latin American immigrants from engaging in mining. As a student of the episode explains,

> Those who opposed Latin Americans in the mines contended that peons [as they were called] lacked a fundamental marker of freedom: a cash wage. Peons were hired men, but the wealthy capitalists who employed them rewarded them only with nonmonetary compensation such as food, goods, and clothing. The cash wage was hardly a hallmark of liberty in antebellum America, a place where most still associated wage labor with dependency and submission. Still, critics of peonage insisted that the absence of cash exchange in the capitalist-peon relationship indicated that Latin American laborers differed markedly from their white American counterparts.[160]

The matter came to a head in the effort to legislate a Civil Rights Act in the 1960s. Initially, the Kennedy administration resisted taking on employment discrimination as a bridge too far on the political map. That hesitance was overcome, and Title VII on employment was added to the 1964 Act even as it was realized at the time that "[b]ringing the Negro to *full economic citizenship* will be a long and complicated undertaking."[161]

The prohibition of discrimination on the grounds of sex had a more complicated history. The demand for equal pay with men doing the same work was advanced from the 1830s[162] through the Gilded Age,[163] the Progressive Period,[164] the New Deal, and into the post-War period. Sex was not included in the initial draft of Title VII of the Civil Rights Act; but, by a circuitous route it was eventually included.[165] Congress was to add other disfavored or marginalized groups for economic inclusion, especially older

members insofar as union business and activity was concerned. James Green, THE DEVIL IS HERE IN THESE HILLS (2015).

159. Hostility to the Chinese was particularly virulent. Even the Knights of Labor were hostile. White, THE REPUBLIC FOR WHICH IT STANDS, *supra* n. 1 at 520-522. Foreign born miners, who made common cause with one another in hard rock mining in the West, were also joined by shared hostility to Chinese workers. Mark Wyman, HARD ROCK EPIC: WESTERN MINERS AND THE INDUSTRIAL REVOLUTION, 1860-1910, Ch. II (1979).
160. Stacey Smith, FREEDOM'S FRONTIER: CALIFORNIA AND THE STRUGGLE OVER UNFREE LABOR, EMANCIPATION, AND RECONSTRUCTION 87-88 (2013). Some actually equated peons lack of a cash wage with actual enslavement. *Id.* at 88.
161. Michael Sovern, LEGAL RESTRAINTS ON RACIAL DISCRIMINATION IN EMPLOYMENT 5 (1966) (italics added). *See also* Paul Norgren & Samuel Hill, TOWARD FAIR EMPLOYMENT (1964).
162. Rockman, SCRAPPING BY, *supra* n. 9 at 150.
163. The Knights of Labor was committed to "equal pay for equal work." Beard, *Knights of Labor*, *supra* n. 26 at 584. Matthew Mark Trumbull, (1826-1894), whose pen name was "Wheelbarrow," reflecting his background as a day laborer, and who became a general in the Civil War, argued for equal workplace rights. Wheelbarrow, ARTICLES AND DISCUSSIONS OF THE LABOR QUESTION 74-76 (1890).
164. Susan Lehrer, ORIGINS OF PROTECTIVE LABOR LEGISLATION FOR WOMEN, 1905-1925, 100 (1987).
165. Alice Kessler-Harris, IN PURSUIT OF EQUITY: WOMEN, MEN, AND THE QUEST FOR ECONOMIC CITIZENSHIP IN THE 20TH CENTURY (2001). Professor Kessler-Harris points out that in 1961, the presidential Executive Order creating the Commission on the Status of Women omitted the word "citizenship" as one of the Commission's goals for the inclusion of women. *Id.* at 215.

persons—eventually resulting in the abolition of mandatory age-based retirement—and persons with disabilities.

These measures were advanced on ethical and on macroeconomic grounds as being beneficial for the economy; but, they were advanced as well on the ground that only by being employed was one a full member of society. The Americans with Disabilities Act was premised on the "right [of the disabled] to fully participate *in all aspects* of society."[166] The rationale for social inclusion was set out in defense of the abolition of mandatory retirement thusly:

> In our society, work is assigned a unique importance. For many, their job is the very bedrock of self-definition. In a very real sense, *we are what we do* .... "The lack of self-maintaining work in old age is therefore a symbol of social failure, a visible justification for the generally inferior social status accorded to the aged in our society."[167]

Many states enacted antidiscrimination laws that transcended the groups protected by federal law; for example, marital status or sexual orientation or identification. Some municipalities did so as well, anticipating the heightened role cities would play in the twenty-first century. The implementation of and practical effect of these federal, state, and municipal anti-discrimination laws and the arguable need for yet more remains one of labor's questions into the twenty-first century.

### *[2] Anti-retaliation*

The Labor Act prohibited employers from retaliating against applicants or employees for having engaged in union or any other concerted activity for mutual aid or protection. Three years later, the Fair Labor Standards Act protected the individual's right to complain of a violation of the law. The right to protest is a feature of any industrial democracy.

Starting with the Civil Rights Act, which protected the individual's right to oppose a practice made unlawful by the Act, the federal and state legislatures began to spin a rich fabric of anti-retaliation laws, some with exacting specificity,[168] protecting the right to complain within the company or to public agencies—"whistleblower" laws. Some laws insulated zones of private action from employer sanction, for example,

166. 42 U.S.C. § 12101(a)(1) (emphasis added).

167. Report of the Select Committee on Aging, Comm. Pub. No. 95-91, 95th Cong., 1st sess. at 23 (Aug. 1977) (emphasis added) (reference omitted). That year the Full Employment and Balanced Growth Act declared as a matter of public policy "the right of every American ... to useful employment paying decent wages." S. Rep. No. 95-1177, 4 U.S. Code Cong. & Admin. News 4398, 4406 (1978).

168. *E.g.* the International Shipping Container Act, 49 U.S.C. § 1501 et seq; the Surface Mining Control and Reclamation Act, 30 U.S.C. § 815(c); the Solid Waste Disposal Act, 42 U.S.C. § 6971; the Energy Reorganization Act, 42 U.S.C. § 5851; and a good deal more.

forbidding discharge for filing for bankruptcy.[169] Three, but, so far, only three states insulate all lawful private life from employer control.[170]

These laws are highly variegated in coverage, procedure, remedies, and effectiveness. They are partial, but only partial measures that accord some legal recognition of the conception of the employee as a bearer of rights capable of being asserted against her employer; they work against the assumption of the relationship as one of tutelage or fealty.[171]

### *[3] Wrongful Dismissal*

By the late 1970s, the at-will rule struck many as harsh and anachronistic.[172] As the next decade progressed, the rule became riddled with exceptions, statutory and judge-made, that varied enormously from state to state. The piling of one exception on after another seemed to call for a coherent law of wrongful dismissal, not only out of fairness but also out of efficiency.[173] In 1991, the National Conference of Commissioners on Uniform State Law considered proposing a uniform state law on wrongful termination but opted instead for a lesser Model Employment Termination Act.[174] To date, no state has enacted it. The state of Montana did adopt a Wrongful Discharge from Employment Act, the only state to move in that direction,[175] but it has had no impact elsewhere. What promised to become a significant labor question in the last

169. 11 U.S.C. § 525(b).

170. Cal. Lab. Code § 98.6; Colo. Rev. Stat. § 24-34-402.5; N.D. Cert. Code § 514-02.4-19. New York protects engagement in "recreational activity." N.Y. Lab. Code § 201–d(2)(c).

171. The chairman of the Board of Directors of General Motors was reported in 1978 to have said of the effort to enact whistleblower protection that, "Some of the enemies of business now encourage an employee to be disloyal to the enterprise." *Quoted in* Andrew Hacker, *Loyalty and the Whistleblower* in INDIVIDUAL RIGHTS IN THE CORPORATION: A READER ON EMPLOYEE RIGHTS 85 (Alan Westin & Stephen Salisbury eds., 1980).

172. Jack Stieber & Michael Murray, *Protection Against Unjust Discharge: The Need for a Federal Statute*, 16 U. Mich. J. L. Reform 319 (1982).

173. *E.g.*, Clyde Summers, *Individual Protection Against Unjust Dismissal: Time for a Statute*, 62 Va. L. Rev. 481 (1976).

174. The proposed law had three fundamental provisions: that employers have to have good cause for dismissal; that the replacement of court trials with arbitration as the preferred method of litigating discharge claims; and that there should be strict limitations on employer liability for wrongful discharge. Employers would be allowed to avoid the good cause requirement by expressly contracting with the employee for severance pay instead. Employees covered by a collective bargaining agreement would be exempt. The law was opposed by trial lawyers who feared the loss of income from the tort claims of their middle class employee-clients. Theodore J. St. Antoine, *The Model Employment Termination Act: A Fair Compromise*, 356 Annals of the American Academy of Political and Social Science 93, 101 (1994).

175. Mont. Code. Ann. § 39-2-901-905. Students of the Montana law report that it has not lived up to its potential. Leonard Bierman, Karen Vinton & Stuart A. Youngblood, *Montana's Wrongful Discharge from Employment Act: The View from the Montana Bar*, 54 MONT. L. REV. 367, 379 (1993). One problem is that often lawyers are unwilling to pursue cases under the law because of the perceived lack of adequate compensation.

quarter of the twentieth century has receded from political contention.[176] Why and whether that should be so will be taken up later.

### [B] Common Law

The state courts were also pressed to adapt the law of contract and tort to late twentieth century notions of job security and fair treatment. In contract, they took a step forward but then took a step back leaving the matter much as it had been before. In tort, the courts began to step forward—then stopped. By century's end, the common law had become frozen.

#### *[1] Contract: Employer Policies on Fair Dismissal*

Before the Second World War, only a small number of firms encouraged long service by placing employees into defined lines of progression and promotion and by offering benefit packages, especially pensions.[177] In the post-War period that all changed: large corporate employers strove to retain workers by commitments to job security, a wide array of company welfare benefits, and internal lines of progression and promotion which combined to create what came to be called "internal labor markets."[178] The shift is illustrated in the compilation and dissemination of employment policies and rules via employee manuals or handbooks.

A small proprietary enterprise does not need employment rules. The owner decides what work to assign, what to pay, whether to permit time off and the like on an ad hoc basis, more or less. But once a company reaches a certain size it needs rules not only to assure conformity with law, it needs to assure evenhanded administration, to govern the discretion of its managers. As of 1935,

> only 13% of industrial firms had adopted employee rulebooks. The bureaucratization of work, however, enmeshes the worker in a "web of rules" and it requires that the rules be known. By 1948, 30% of industrial firms had adopted employee handbooks. A 1979 survey of 6,000 companies revealed that employee handbooks were distributed by approximately 75% of the companies responding.[179]

The common assumption was that these policies were meant to be relied on by both management and employees. As a personnel advisory in 1984 put it, "Say only what you mean. If your handbook contains phrases such as 'permanent employee' or

---

176. Not necessarily from the public forum. *See* Moshe Marvit & Shaun Richman, *A Better Way to Protect Workers*, N.Y. Times, Dec. 29, 2017 at A-25 (arguing for wrongful dismissal law).
177. The richly textured history is explored by Sanford Jacoby, Employing Bureaucracy: Managers, Unions, and the Transformation of Work in American Industry, 1900-1945 (1985).
178. *See* Internal Labor Markets (Paul Osterman, ed. 1984); *see also* Sanford Jacoby, Modern Manors: Welfare Capitalism Since the New Deal (1997).
179. Matthew Finkin, *The Bureaucratization of Work: Employer Policies and Contract Law*, 1986 Wis. L. Rev. 733, 743 (1986) (references omitted).

'discharge for good cause,' consider it a contractual commitment to employees, just as *some* courts have."[180]

As the emphasized portion of the advisory implies, the courts had not yet settled on the legal status of these instruments. Initially, the courts had a difficult time fitting them into the common law's doctrinal requirements for contract—of individual offer and acceptance, of a bargain that reflects a meeting of the minds of the bargaining partners. Eventually, it became generally recognized that employer rules on job security and the imposition of discipline could be legally binding by virtue of dissemination alone. But, in the same breath, the courts took the position that a sufficiently conspicuous and clearly worded disclaimer of contractual effect would be legally operative. Thus an employer could at once give an express assurance of fair treatment and simultaneously take away the legal ground on which it could be enforced. Unsurprisingly, the American legal establishment has given this its stamp of approval.[181]

### *[2] Tort: Wrongful Dismissal*

The prospect of there being a judge-made limit to the law-free zone the courts created in the Gilded Age's at-will rule was hinted at in 1959 when a California court held it tortious to discharge an employee for refusing to commit perjury.[182] Cases increasingly pressed the theory that the power to discharge cannot be used to sanction an employee who was acting in pursuit of a public purpose.[183] The courts differed on what public policies were sufficiently strong to truncate the power to discharge and even what sources could be looked to as providing a governing policy.

Two approaches emerged. The first gathered the jurisdiction's case law over the previous decades and assembled them into categories. In other words, the cases were put into boxes,[184] many or few depending on the jurisdiction's experience. The effect was to freeze the law as of the time of categorization. If a case later arose that did not fit into one of the established boxes, it would have an uphill struggle to be actionable. The second took a more open-ended approach that potentially invited new sources of policy to be examined and applied.[185]

At the century's turn, the American legal establishment gave its stamp of approval to the former: it surveyed the boxes the more narrowly focused states had

180. Personnel Management: Policies and Practices (P-H) ¶ 21, 214 (1984) (italics added).
181. American Law Institute, Restatement of the Law of Employment § 2.05 cmt. c, Illustration 2 (2015). The ALI's product has been critically assessed by Stephen Befort, *Employee Handbooks and Policy Statements: From Gratuities to Contracts and Back Again*, 21 Employee Rts. & Emp. Pol'y J. 307 (2017).
182. Petermann v. Int'l Bhd. Teamsters, 344 P.3d 25 (Cal. App. 1959).
183. By the mid to late 1980s, there was a substantial accumulation of case law. *See* Annot., 9 ALR 4th 330 (1981) and 12 ALR 4th 544 (1982).
184. *E.g.* Mikhail v. Penn. Org. for Women and Early Recovery, 63 A.3d 313 (Pa. Super. 2013).
185. *E.g.*, Blackburn v. American Rental Centers, 22 N.E.3d 1149 (Ohio App. 2014). These courts have relied on factors set out by Henry Perritt, Jr., Workplace Torts: Rights and Liabilities §§ 3.7, 3.14, 3.19, 3.21 (1991).

created and endorsed a set of categories of its own, which, if the effort proves influential, would set the law in stone.[186]

## §4.04 AT CENTURY'S END: LABOR SEGMENTATION AND POLARIZATION, BUSINESS FISSURIZATION, UNION IMPLOSION, AND THE PRIVATIZATION OF LAW

The last quarter of the twentieth century witnessed the disintegration of the post-War model.[187] Jobs shifted from manufacturing to services, from blue to white collar work and to further segmentation within services to a bi-modal distribution of well-paid professional and technical jobs and low waged jobs in food, leisure, health care and other services. Some vertically integrated business disintegrated down fissured chains of subcontracting abetted by computer technology. Union density went into steep decline. Wages for the lower deciles of the workforce fell, the middle tiers stagnated. Only the top decile held its own, with the top 1% doing well. More risk was shifted to employees: the risk of anticipating change in needed skills and being retrained in them; the risk of not being supported by a sufficient income in post-working years. Management was allowed to require such protections as the law afforded to be submitted exclusively to arbitration systems of the company's devising, the confidentiality of which insulated one employee's claim from another and shielded the results from public scrutiny. These developments set the stage for the next century. Each is sketched in below.

### [A] Labor Segmentation and Polarization

The change in the nature of jobs the economy generated, 1940-2009, is set out in Table 4.1.

186. Am. Law Inst., Restatement of the Law: Employment Law § 5.02 (2015). Another option was available. It is a common law principle that all contracts are instinct with an implied obligation of good faith and fair dealing. If the employment relationship is one of contract, it would seem that this obligation would apply not only to limit employer opportunism—discharging an employee to avoid the accrual of a benefit—but to all other employer action taken in bad faith, or arbitrarily insofar as such would be an element of fair dealing. That would have the law constrain employer prerogative without connection to any other public policy. The vast majority of American courts have rejected it. As a result, the American rule is that all contracts, including employment contracts of fixed duration, are instinct with an obligation of good faith, *except* contracts of at-will employment. The American legal establishment has put its stamp of approval on this as well, cabining good faith to a narrowly confined area of application. *Id.* § 2.07. For a critique of the ALI's product *see* Lea Vander Velde, *Where is the Concept of Good Faith in the Restatement of Employment?*, 21 Employee Rts. & Emp. Pol'y J. 335 (2017).

187. Charles Sabel, Work and Politics: The Division of Labor in Industry Ch. 5 (1982) ("The End of Fordism?"); David Gordon, Richard Edwards & Michael Reich, Segmented Work, Divided Workers: The Historical Transformation of Labor in the United States (1982).

*Table 4.1 Composition of the Labor Force by Job Type*

| | *1940* | *1970* | *2009* |
|---|---|---|---|
| Blue collar | 38.2% | 35.8% | 19.9% |
| White collar | 28.3% | 37.7% | 41.4% |
| Sales | 6.3% | 7.2% | 11.6% |
| Non-domestic Services | 7.2% | 11.0% | 17.1% |
| Professional | 7.2% | 15.5% | 20.7% |

*Source*: Robert Gordon, THE RISE AND FALL OF AMERICAN GROWTH TABLE 8-1 at p. 255 (2016).

The white collar services sector includes both high-end jobs, many of which are separated out in the above as professional in nature, usually salaried and offering a package of benefits, which category has nearly trebled since 1940, and low-wage workers—those paid at or close to the minimum wage. In other words, since about 1970, the share of well-paid high skilled jobs and low paid low skilled jobs has increased while the share of middle-skilled middle-paid jobs has declined. This shift has been termed "job polarization."[188] The explanation for and consequences of it will be taken up at the close.

With respect to the low-wage job distribution, in 2013 the labor force included 75.3 million hourly paid workers of which the cohort paid minimum wage (or below) constituted 4.7%. These major categories constituting these jobs are set out below.[189] Half of these workers are between 16 and 24; that is, half are 25 or older; most are white (78%), most are women, and most work part-time (64%). But if the focus expands to workers making only 25 cents an hour *above* the minimum wage, the cohort expands to 5.5 million workers, or 7.3% of the hourly paid workforce: three quarters of this

188. David Autor, Laurence Katz & Melissa Kennedy, *The Polarization of the U.S. Labor Market*, 96 Am. Econ. Rev. 89 (2006).

189.

**Selected Minimum Wage Workers by Occupational Group, 2012**

| *Occupational Group* | *Workforce* |
|---|---|
| Food preparation and serving related occupations | 1,555,000 |
| Sales and related occupations | 546,000 |
| Personal care and service occupations | 268,000 |
| Transportation and material moving occupations | 240,000 |
| Building and grounds cleaning and maintenance occupations | 231,000 |
| Office and administrative support occupations | 227,000 |

*Source*: PEW Research Center, *Who makes minimum wage?* (July 19, 2013).

cohort is over 20 years old; 40% work full time.[190] Even the low-wage segment is further segmented into groups with quite separate concerns that might have call for specific legal address, such as workers dependent on customer tips.

The segmentation of jobs since the 1970s was accompanied by a widening wage inequality. There is no doubt that those with a four-year college degree fare better—in wages and in the risk of long-term unemployment—than those with only a high school education or less,[191] but there has also been a growing wage inequality within occupations.[192]

The labor market also further segmented workers by work arrangement. The U.S. Bureau of Labor Statistics conducted two surveys—one for 2005, one for 2017. The results are summarized below.

*Table 4.2 Nonstandard Workers in the U.S. 2005*

| | *All* | *Women* | *Men* |
|---|---|---|---|
| Standard workers | 69.4% | 64.8% | 73.5% |
| Nonstandard workers | 30.6% | 35.2% | 26.5% |
| Select categories of nonstandard workers | | | |
| Regular part-time | 13.2 | 19.0 | 7.9 |
| Direct hire temporaries | 2.1 | 2.3 | 2.0 |
| Temp agency | 0.9 | 1.0 | 0.8 |
| Independent contractor (self-employed) | 6.5 | 4.6 | 8.2 |
| On-call/day laborers | 2.0 | 2.0 | 2.0 |

*Source*: Lawrence Mishel, Jared Bernstein, & Heidi Shierholz, THE STATE OF WORKING AMERICA 2008/2009 Table 4.7 at p. 253 (2009). A "standard worker" works more than 35 hours per week and is not paid by a staffing firm.

*Table 4.3 Contingent and Alternative Employment in the U.S. (2017)*

| *Category* | *Number (million)* | *% of Total Employment* |
|---|---|---|
| Independent contractors | 10.6 | 6.9% |
| Temp Agency & Contract Workers | 2.3 | 1.5% |
| On-call | 2.6 | 1.7% |

*Source*: BLS Contingent and Alternative Employment Arrangements Survey—May 2017 (June 7, 2018).

190. Congressional Budget Office, The Effects of a Minimum-Wage Increase on Employment and Family Income 4 (Feb. 2014).
191. Lawrence Mischel, Josh Bivens, Elise Gould & Heidi Shierholz, THE STATE OF WORKING AMERICA Ch. 4 (12th ed. 2012) ("Wages: The top, and very top, outpace the rest.")
192. John Schmidt, Heidi Shierholz & Lawrence Mischel, Don't Blame the Robots: Assessing the Job Polarization Explanation of Growing Wage Inequality, EPI Report (Nov. 2013).

Annette Bernhardt has pointed out that, in terms of the distribution of nonstandard work by certain characteristics—sex, age, part-time as compared to full-time and the like—rather little has changed. The decline in the display of nonstandard work would appear surprising given the speculation on the likely rise in independent contractors and those in contingent work arrangements as a result of the "on-demand" or "gig" economy.[193] But, she cautions that there is much the survey does not pick up: full-time workers who act as independent contractors to supplement their income; workers so subject to precarious work schedules as effectively to be on-call, but who are not included in the survey's definition of on-call work; and more. Even by its more restrictive approach, in 2017, at least 3.8% of the workforce—5.9 million workers—were contingent.

### [B] Business Fissurization

The term was coined by David Weil.[194] What it means was summarized in the introduction to a collection of papers appearing in the *Comparative Labor Law & Policy Journal.*[195] The editors started with Weil's explanation:

> During much of the twentieth century, the critical employment relationship was between large businesses and workers. Large businesses with national and international reputations operating at the top of their industries continue to focus on delivering value to their customers and investors. However, most no longer directly employ legions of workers to make products or deliver services. Employment has been actively shed by these market leaders and transferred to a complicated network of smaller business units. Lower-level businesses operate in more highly competitive markets than those of the firms that shifted employment to them.[196]

As the editors explain, this reverses the way business was "wired" in the post-War period of consolidation:

> Wage setting and supervision shift from core businesses to a myriad of organizations, each operating under the rigorous standards of lead businesses but facing fierce competitive pressures. Although lead businesses set demanding goals and standards, and often detailed work practice requirements for subsidiary companies, the actual liability, oversight, and supervision of the workforce become the problem of one or more other organizations. And by replacing a direct employment

193. Annette Bernhardt, Making Sense of the New Government Data on Contingent Work, https://blog.usejournal.com/making-sense-of-the-new-government-data-on-contingent-work097209bb0c615.

194. David Weil, The Fissured Workplace: Why Work Became So Bad for So Many and What Can Be Done to Improve It (2014).

195. *Symposium in Honor of Bob Hepple: The Fissured Workplace*, 37 Comp. Lab. L. & Pol'y J. No. 1 (2015). A parallel set of papers was sponsored by the Japan Institute of Labor Policy and Training, *The Notion of the Employer in the Era of the Fissured Workplace*, Bull. Comp. Lab. Rel. No. 95 (Hiroya Nakakubo & Takashi Araki, eds. 2017).

196. Weil, *supra* n. 194 at 8.

relationship with a fissured workplace, employment itself becomes more precarious, with risk shifted onto smaller employers and individual workers, who are often cast in the role of independent businesses in their own right.[197]

Fissurization increases the prospect of wage theft by subcontractors and contributes to greater wage inequality. Weil uses franchising as an illustration. He shows that company-owned outlets are much less susceptible to the commission of wage and hour violations than are franchisees. In 2018, there were almost 760,000 franchised establishments in the U.S. employing about 8,200,000 workers.[198]

Another way work can be fissured is by crafting the terms of employment in such a way as to cause the worker to be categorized as an independent contractor and not an employee. Disputes over characterization have become ubiquitous; many states have enacted mischaracterization statutes to sanction willful attempts to avoid labor protection—and state taxes. Exemplar One boils down considerably the extensive contract terms governing package deliverymen in which that attempt was made.

**Exemplar One**

**FedEx Home Delivery Standard Contractor Operating Agreement**

(June 2006)

*The* Standard Contractor Operating Agreement *consumes twenty-six single spaced pages and several detailed Addenda. Whether the persons executing it were employees or independent contractors was litigated before the National Labor Relations Board, to determine whether they were statutory employees eligible to engage in collective bargaining, and before several state courts to determine whether they were statutory employees entitled to wage and hour protections under their state laws. The key elements of the Agreement were summarized by the Labor Board in* FedEx Home Delivery, *361 NLRB No. 55 (2014).*

*General provisions*. The agreement is offered on a take it or leave it basis though the driver can have the agreement reviewed by a lawyer or accountant. It provides that the driver serves "strictly as an independent contractor, and not as an employee of FHD for any purpose." The agreement is for a fixed period, one or two years, subject to renewal on 30 days' notice of non-renewal. Summary termination is also provided for in the event *inter alia* of misconduct, which can be taken to arbitration.

197. *Introduction to The Fissured Workplace*, 37 Comp. Lab. L. & Pol'y J. 3, 4 (2015). David Leonhardt, a business columnist for the New York Times, has drawn on the Census Bureau's Business Dynamics Statistics and concluded that the share of American workers' who work for large companies has increased since 1985 to 2014, the last year for which data are available: there has been a decline on average of about 3% of those who work for companies with fewer than 100 workers; an increase of about 2% in those working for companies of between 100 and 1,000 workers; and an increase of 3% in those working for companies with 10,000 or more workers. David Leonhardt, *The Charts Show How Big Business is Winning*, https://www.nytimes/com/2018/06/17/opinion-big-business-mergers.html. I have been cautioned by an academic economist that there are difficulties of working with that particular data set.

198. Int'l Franchise Ass'n: HIS Market Statistics (2018).

*Vehicles*. The driver must purchase a vehicle subject to FedEx's approval. FedEx does not provide financing. FedEx requires that the vehicles be white, have a backing camera, and be maintained in a clean condition, free of damages or extraneous markings. All vehicles display the FedEx logo. Drivers bear all expenses in operating their vehicles, including costs of repair, maintenance, fuel, oil, taxes, tires, insurance, and license fees. When the vehicle is in the service of FedEx, "it shall be used by [the driver] exclusively for the carriage of the goods of FHD, and for no other purpose." At all other times, drivers may use their vehicles for other commercial or personal purposes provided they remove or mask FedEx's logos.

*Route Acquisition*. Routes are obtained from FedEx at no cost to the drivers but they may also require routes from other drivers. However, FedEx is allowed to reconfigure routes.

*Responsibilities*. The Agreement requires the drivers to make their schedules available for delivery on enumerated days and hours. All packages must be delivered the same day the packages arrive. The drivers must wear FedEx uniforms and badges maintained in good condition and adhere to FedEx's grooming standards. After each delivery the driver must input the data into a scanner which also records off-duty time. The data system is used to monitor driver performance. Specific rules govern the making of deliveries, customer acceptance, whether customers are at home, and the like. FedEx maintains the right to conduct driver audits including "ride along" inspections by management. Otherwise, drivers are free to deliver in the order they think best or take breaks so long as the work is completed. FedEx retains the right to adjust the drivers' volume of packages or to require them to deliver packages outside their routes.

*Compensation*. Drivers are paid on the basis of the number of packages delivered, stops made, distance traveled, days of availability, and the like. Bonuses are also paid. FedEx provides financial support in the event of significant fuel cost increases and for it to pay certain vehicle related costs. However, it does not provide for vacations, paid holidays, or other fringe benefits. It does not collect taxes.

*Insurance*. Drivers are required to carry insurance for general liability, vehicle damage, and work accidents.

*Hiring of supplemental drivers and helpers*: A driver can hire as a substitute a DOT-qualified and FedEx-approved driver or, in response to an increase in the volume of work, hire such a person to work another leased vehicle as a supplemental driver.
*Route sales*:

> Drivers may also sell their routes to buyers deemed qualified by FedEx and willing to enter into the Agreement with FedEx "on substantially the same terms and conditions" as the original driver. Although drivers need not receive FedEx's permission regarding a pending route sale, FedEx must be notified once the sale is

complete so that the buyer can sign the Agreement. FedEx is not involved in the negotiations between the parties, but it retains the right to approve the individual.

The National Labor Relations Board held the drivers to be employees, but the U.S. Court of Appeals for the District of Columbia Circuit disagreed. It found the drivers' opportunity for "entrepreneurial activity"—the sale of their routes—to be dispositive even if almost never availed of and even though FedEx could render the sale worthless.[199] If this view prevails, either because the Supreme Court will endorse it or because the Labor Board, now controlled by an employer-friendly administration, agrees, FedEx cannot be required to bargain with its drivers over their rates of pay, hours, or vehicular costs.

Federal and, perhaps more importantly, state wage and hour law often looks more closely to that which distinguishes a true business relationship from one of employment, sometimes by application of a statutory "suffer or permit to work" test. Under that provision, California has adopted an "ABC" test in which all of three factors must be met in order for the worker to be held to be an independent contractor: (a) that the worker is free from control in the performance of the work; (b) that the work is outside the usual course of the business for which the work is performed; and (c) that the worker is customarily engaged in an independently established trade or business.[200] Massachusetts and New Jersey have adopted this test.[201] Kansas, however, has embraced an amalgam of economic realities and right to control as its test of status.[202] Even then, FedEx's drivers were held to be employees. At the close of an exacting twenty-two page, factor-by-factor analysis the Kansas Supreme Court summed it up thusly,

> FedEx has established an employment relationship with its delivery drivers but dressed that relationship in independent contractor clothing. Even where the factors should point us toward finding that the drivers are independent businesspersons, FedEx's control and micromanaging undermine the benefit that a driver should be able to reap from that arrangement. For instance, the ability to make more money than a delivery driver who is an employee is diminished, if not destroyed, by FedEx's control over the deliveries a driver can make, as well as essentially dictating the driver's required expenditures for vehicles, tools, equipment, and clothing.[203]

Consequently, in California, New Jersey, Kansas, and elsewhere FedEx drivers can demand the protection that state law provides for their extant wages; but, they may not be able to bargain to increase their wages. It is a commonplace that the same word may have different meanings for the purposes of different laws; but, given the purposes of these laws, something certainly seems seriously amiss.

199. FedEx Home Delivery v. NLRB, 840 F.3d 1123 (D.C. Cir. 2017).
200. Dynamex Operations West, Inc. v. Superior Court, 4 Cal. 5th 903 (2018).
201. The former by statute. Mass. Gen. L. c149, §148D. The latter by judicial extension. Hargrove v. Sleepy's LLC, 106 A.3d 449 (N.J. 2015).
202. Craig v. FedEx Ground Package Sys., Inc. 335 P.3d 66 (Kan. 2014).
203. *Id.* at 92.

The question of classification has taken on added salience due to the resort at century's end to "gig" or "crowdsourced" work of which Uber and Lyft have been most prominent but which includes all manner of work given out by or through companies operating electronic platforms. What the labor questions are that these businesses forms generate will be taken up later.

### [C] Union Implosion

In 1973, private sector union density stood at about 25%, down from about 35% in the 1950s. Today, it is about 6.6%. This has had significant economic consequences insofar as union agreements no longer set a standard that nonunion enterprises emulate to remain nonunion.[204] In the era of union strength, a tacit trade-off was made that had broader economic consequences: labor agreed to become more productive, and productivity-enhancing technology was introduced without great turmoil;[205] but, labor realized the benefit of increased productivity by increased wages. In other words, wage growth would parallel productivity growth. The tacit understanding disintegrated once unions started to decline in the late 1970s as Figure 4.1 evidences.

*Figure 4.1 Cumulative Change in Total Economy Productivity and Real Hourly Compensation of Production/Nonsupervisory Workers, 1948-2011*

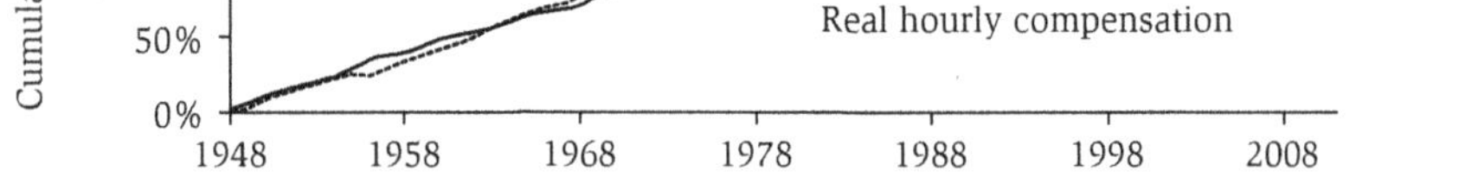


*Source*: Laurence Mischel, Josh Bivens, Elise Gould & Heidi Shierholz, THE STATE OF WORKING AMERICA, Figure 4U at p. 236 (12th ed. 2012).

204. *See generally*, Jake Rosenfeld, WHAT UNIONS NO LONGER DO (2014).
205. From the left, this has been seen as a sell-out. David Gartman, AUTO SLAVERY: THE LABOR PROCESS IN THE AMERICAN AUTOMOBILE INDUSTRY, 1879-1950, 269-270 (1986):

> Automotive manufacturers demanded from the union above all a stable, predictable, and compliant work force to work their machines and valorize their capital. In return, they were willing to ensure the organization's survival, as well as make concessions in the areas of wages, benefits, hours of work, seniority, and other employment conditions.

The result has been a widening wage inequality, a stark reversal of the trend in the immediate post-War decades. Those years may have been abberrational,[206] but the consequence of the trend toward inequality over the last several decades has exceeded the inequality in the distribution of earned income at the end of the Gilded Age. Table 3.1 set out the comparison of earned income distribution in the U.S. 1918 to 2010. But earned income is but one component of household wealth. The political and social consequences of disparities the distribution of wealth were discussed earlier.[207] This can be put into sharper historical relief if we compare the Florentine Republic with the American.

*Table 4.4 Household Wealth Distribution in Florence 1427 and the U.S. 2010( % of Total Wealth (Rounded))*

| *Wealth Bracket* | *Florence* | *U.S.* |
|---|---|---|
| Top 1% | 27 | 35.4 |
| Top 5% | 54 | 63.1 |
| Top 10% | 69 | 76.7 |
| Top 20% | 84 | 88.9 |

*Source*: For Florence, Richard Goldthwaite, THE ECONOMY OF RENAISSANCE FLORENCE Table 7.3 (2009); for the U.S., Edward N. Wolff, THE ASSET PRICE MELTDOWN AND THE WEALTH OF THE MIDDLE CLASS (NBER Working Paper No. 18559) (Nov. 2012).

The decline in private sector union density is the product of a variety of factors, economic and demographic, but legal academics sympathetic to collective bargaining have added deficiencies in the Labor Act into the mix. As noted earlier, given the tepid nature of remedies under the Act, the realization of effective employee workplace voice—which in the 1930s strode under the banner of "industrial democracy"—depends on active employee engagement and, when needed, by self-help, a capacity and willingness to impose a significant cost of disagreement on employers; that is, traditionally, a strike. But as Figure 4.2 shows, there has been a significant diminution in strike activity in last quarter century, a diminution that far exceeds the deadline in union density and so cannot be attributed to it.

206. The point made by Robert Gordon, THE RISE AND FALL OF AMERICAN GROWTH: THE U.S. STANDARD OF LIVING SINCE THE CIVIL WAR (2016) and placed in larger historical context by Walter Scheidel, THE GREAT LEVELER (2017).

207. See the text accompanying *supra* n. 40.

*Figure 4.2 Union Membership and Strike Activity 1990–2015*

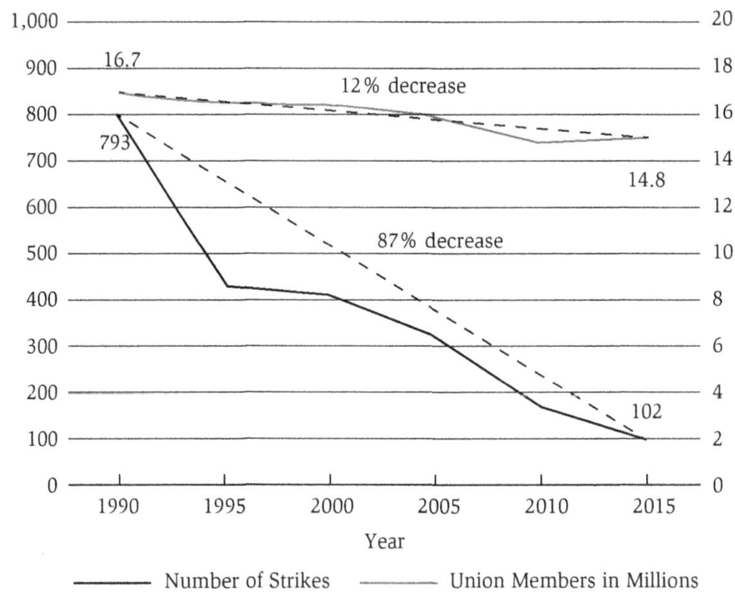


*Source*: Bloomberg Law, BNA Labor PLUS Data.

Two caveats about Figure 4.2. First, union membership data includes the public sector, hence the overall union density shown of about 13.5% instead of 6.6% in the private sector. However, most of the states that permit public employees to bargain collectively do not allow them to strike. Second, in the 1980s the federal government ceased to compile strike data for strikes involving fewer than a thousand workers. Thus the figure will not reflect smaller walk-outs. Even so, even taken as only a rough indication, the decline in self-help is beyond dispute. This opens the question of whether there is more that law should do.

## §4.05 THE PRIVATIZATION OF LABOR PROTECTIVE LAW

In 1925, Congress legislated against the reluctance of the courts to enforce agreements to arbitrate future disputes. It passed what came to be called the Federal Arbitration Act (FAA). Arbitration provisions in transactions over which Congress had jurisdiction, involving foreign or interstate commerce, were made "valid, irrevocable, and enforceable, save upon such grounds as exist at law or in equity for the revocation of any contract."[208] The Court's engagement with the law started from the obvious proposition that it placed contracts to arbitrate on an equal footing as all other contracts—no

208. 9 U.S.C. §2.

less, but no more—and the Supreme Court said as much.[209] Starting in the late 1980s, however, the Court became ever more enchanted with arbitration.[210] Questions of public law could be submitted for arbitral disposition on a theory of forum substitution which the court had rejected decades before.[211] In a bizarre decision, the Act's exclusion of workers' contracts from the law was held, five to four, to exclude only these workers over whom Congress had jurisdiction in 1925, that is employees who crossed a state border in the conduct of their work. All employees over whom Congress had no jurisdiction at the time and for whom it could not legislate but over whom it now had jurisdiction, by virtue of the Court's rereading of the Commerce Clause in the 1930s, were held to be included.[212] Employers were quick to react.

Exemplar Two is edited down from the seven single-spaced page policy governing employees of Ernst & Young U.S., a managerial consulting firm. It was selected to give an idea of the detail such policies may go into and because the section set out in bold print was to go before the U.S. Supreme Court.

**Exemplar Two**

Ernst & Young Common Ground Dispute Resolution Program

*Effective as of May 1, 2006*

I. Preamble

The Common Ground Dispute Resolution Program, as outlined in this document (the "Program"), is intended to provide a fair, prompt, and cost-effective mechanism for resolving disputes. The Program is the sole method for resolving disputes within its coverage. It is not intended to limit or expand substantive rights that would otherwise be available under law.

II. Coverages of Program

A. *Entities and persons covered.*

***

2. "Employee" means an applicant for employment or an employee of the Firm who is bound by the terms and conditions of the Program ....

B. *Disputes covered.*

1. All claims, controversies, or other disputes between the Firm and an Employee that could otherwise be resolved by a court, except as stated below ("Covered Disputes"), shall be resolved through the Program. Both

209. Prima Paint Corp. v. Flood & Conklin Mfg. Co. 388 U.S. 395, n. 12 at 404 (1967); Sheik v. Alberto-Culver Co., 417 U.S. 506, 511 (1974).
210. The story has been described as one of a love affair. Matthew Finkin, *L'arbitrage aux États-Unis, une véritable histoire d'amour*, Droit Social 128 (Férrier 2017).
211. Gilmer v. Interstate/Johnson Lane Corp., 5000 U.S. 20 (1991).
212. Circuit City Stores, Inc. v. Adams, 532 U.S. 105 (2001).

the Firm and the Employee give up any right to resolve any Covered Dispute through any other means. *Neither the Firm nor an Employee will be able to sue in court in connection with a Covered Dispute.*

***

C. *Examples of types of disputes covered.* Examples of Covered Disputes include:

1. Claims based on federal statutes such as Title VII of the Civil Rights Act of 1964, the Civil Rights Act of 1991, the Age Discrimination in Employment Act, the Americans with Disabilities Act, the Fair Labor Standards Act, the Equal Pay Act, the Rehabilitation Act of 1973, the Family and Medical Leave Act, the Employee Retirement Income Security Act and the Worker Adjustment and Retraining Notification Act, all as have been or may be amended.

2. Claims based on state statutes and local ordinances, including state and local antidiscrimination laws.

3. Claims based on common law theories such as tort and contract.

***

*These examples are not exclusive and are provided only as examples of some of the kinds of Covered Disputes that may exist. All Covered Disputes, whether or not listed here, must be resolved through the Program.*

III. Phase I — Mediation

***

IV. Phase II — Arbitration

***

D. *Arbitration Rules.* The arbitration will be conducted in accordance with the Program and the relevant arbitration rules of the Provider as in effect on the Effective Date ("Arbitration Rules"). The relevant rules may be viewed here (for CPR), here (AAA), and here (JAMS). If there is any conflict between the Arbitration Rules and the Program, the Program will take precedence.

E. *Initiation.*

***

F. *Attorney Representation.* Either party may choose to be represented by a lawyer in the arbitration, or may choose not to use a lawyer.

G. *Number of Selection of Arbitrators:*

***

H. *Arbitrator Competence.* Any issue about whether a claim, controversy or dispute is subject to arbitration, or about how the terms and conditions of the Program should be interpreted or whether they are binding on the parties, will be decided by the Arbitrator.

I. *Venue....*

J. *Law Applicable to Arbitration.* In deciding a Covered Dispute, the Arbitrator will apply the substantive law, including burdens of proof, that would be applied by a court in the venue of the arbitration. The Arbitrator may grant any relief that could be granted by such a court, but will have no power to grant any other relief.

***

K. *Separate Proceedings.* If there is more than one Covered Dispute between the Firm and an Employee, all such Covered Disputes may be heard in a single proceeding. **Covered Disputes pertaining to different Employees will be heard in separate proceedings.** *[Bold added.]*

L. *Discovery....*

M. *Witnesses....*

N. *Summary Adjudication....*

O. *Conduct of Hearing....*

P. *Fees and Expenses....*

***

2. *Arbitrator fees and other costs.* The parties intent is for Arbitrator fees and other costs of the arbitration, other than filing and administrative fees, to be shared equally to the extent permitted by law and the Arbitration Rules. However, the portion of the cost to be paid by an Employer will be adjusted to the extent, if any, necessary for the parties' agreement to arbitrate be enforced.

***

Q. *Award.* The Arbitrator shall render an award and written opinion in the form typically rendered in labor arbitrations....

V. Other Matters

A. *Confidentiality.* All aspects...including any award made, shall be confidential, except to the extent disclosure is required by law or applicable professional standards, or is necessary in a later proceeding between the parties.

B. *At-Will Employment.* The Program does not change the at-will status of Employees and does not create any contract between an Employee and the Firm, other than as to those matters expressly addressed in the Program.

***

E. *Termination or Amendment.*

***

F. *Due Process and Severability.*

1. The Program is intended to be fair to both sides and to provide access by employees at an affordable cost. If it is determined that all or part of the Program is unenforceable for reasons pertaining to the fairness of the procedures or the cost, the Firm shall have the option to modify the Program as appropriate to address the concern.

2. If any portion of the Program is held to be invalid or unenforceable, or if any portion of the Program would, if effective, violate applicable law, that portion of the program shall be void and of no effect, but the remainder of the Program shall remain in full force and effect.

G. *Choice of Law Governing Program.* The Program, these procedures, and any arbitration award that may result from them shall be governed by the Federal Arbitration Act and to the extent, if any, that such Act is held not to apply, to the state law, including judicial interpretations, applicable in the State of New York, provided that principles of conflicts of laws shall not be applied.

Today, about 25 to 30% of the private sector workforce is covered by such arbitration provisions. Research has revealed the consequences: on average, employees win less often in arbitration than in court and are awarded less; employees represent themselves a bit more often—about 5% more—than in court, but employees who are represented by lawyers do better in arbitration than those who represent themselves; the lawyers who represent employers in arbitration are more experienced in employment law than those who represent employees; lawyers are less likely to take cases where the forum is restricted to arbitration; those arbitrators who are selected frequently by employers—employers being repeat players in the system whereas the individual employee is not—tend to decide cases more often for employers.[213]

Further, unlike judicial proceedings arbitration is confidential. This is so by the rules of the listing agencies and can be echoed in the terms of the employer's policy, just as Ernst & Young's does in section V(A). This means that the evidence adduced in one case would not be available to the employee arbitrating the same issue arising out of the same event in another case. The benefit for employers who are the repeat players is palpable. Moreover, because not only the process but also the arbitrator's judgments

213. David Horton & Andrea Chandrasekher, *Employment Arbitration after the Revolution*, 65 Depaul L. Rev. 457 (2016); Alexander J.S. Colvin & Mark Gough, *Individual Employment Rights Arbitration in the United States: Actors and Outcomes*, 68 ILR Rev. 1010 (2015); Alexander J.S. Colvin, *Mandatory Arbitration and Inequality of Justice in Employment*, 35 Berk. J. Emp. & Lab. L. 71 (2014).

are confidential, the public has no way of knowing whether the laws are being faithfully enforced. The law will have disappeared from public view.[214]

Note that the Ernst & Young policy provides that disputes "pertaining to different Employees will be heard in separate proceedings." This, even if the facts and issues presented in them are identical: for example of two employees or twenty or a hundred who complain in common of a manager's order or a company policy that results in wage theft or misclassification. In the commercial area, the Supreme Court had found bilateral arbitration—a dispute that has only one claimant—to be a "fundamental" attribute of what arbitration under the FAA meant grounded only in the Court's say that it is so, for nothing in the statutes speaks to it. As a result, consumers can be precluded by boilerplate arbitration contracts from bringing or participating in a class or group claim about their purchases: arbitration agreements allowing only for individual arbitrations must be enforced, the Court said, "as written."

Here, too, employers were quick to get the cue. Unlike commercial transactions, however, labor law would seem to speak to such a restriction: the Norris-LaGuardia Act prohibits the federal courts from enforcing any "understanding or promise" by which employees eschew the capacity to join one another in a labor dispute, to engage in concerted activity for mutual aid or protection; the Labor Act forbids employees from exacting such understandings or promises. The National Labor Relations Board held to just that effect, but the courts of appeals divided on the question. The U.S. Supreme Court consolidated three cases—*Ernst & Young*, *Epic Systems*, and *Murphy Oil*—and, by a five-to-four vote, the majority, in an opinion authored by Justice Neil Gorsuch, held the preclusion to control.[215]

The texture of the debate between Justice Gorsuch and Justice Ginsburg writing for the dissent is too rich even to summarize. It is enough only to note three critical aspects: doctrinal coherence, historical faithfulness, and practical consequences.

First, on doctrinal coherence, Justice Gorsuch argues that the Labor Act's overwhelming concern was with unionization and collective bargaining—which is true—and that the inclusion of "other concerted activity" was merely a "catch-all" on which accordingly too much weight should not be placed. As we have seen, however, the Court seemed to place considerable weight on it in the *Eastex*[216] case for it was under that clause that workers were held to have a right in the workplace to circulate literature supporting an increase in the minimum wage, as an exercise of their right collectively to seek redress in a forum outside the immediate work relationship for the protection of their workplace rights. That right would apply equally to nonunion workers: the basis of the decision had nothing to do with unionization and everything to do with concerted activity for mutual aid or protection. To this, Justice Gorsuch replied that all the Court's talk in *Eastex* about workers seeking collective redress in other fora was just that—talk, language not essential to the holding in the case, "dicta." Run the scenario of nonunion workers circulating a minimum wage petition in their

214. Matthew Finkin, *Workplace Justice: Does Private Judging Matter?*, ZVglR Wiss 113 (2014) 166.
215. Epic Sys. Corp. v. Lewis, 138 S.Ct. 1612 (2018).
216. See the text accompanying *supra* n. 138.

workplace and ask: Can their employer prohibit them from doing so?[217] If it may not—and it may not—it would be because of statutory dictate, not judicial dictum.

Nevertheless, put the Labor Act aside. What about Norris-LaGuardia? What about it?, Gorsuch replies. It "adds nothing" as it simply adumbrates the policy the Labor Act adopts. This is a classic case of circular reasoning. It does not follow that because the labor act of 1935 was principally concerned with unionization and collective bargaining, the Norris-LaGuardia Act of 1932 was similarly fixated.

This leads into the second arresting aspect of Justice Gorsuch's opinion: its lack of historical faithfulness. Recall that an evil the Norris-LaGuardia Act targeted was the Yellow Dog Contract. Recall that yellow dogs, albeit of the same color came in sundry forms the common attribute of which was the atomization of the workforce, the negation of the capacity of workers to band together, to summon or go to one another's aid. These came in such variety that two monographs of the period attempted to catalog them. Joel Seidman's study noted the policy of the street railway company in Baltimore that required workers to "arbitrate all differences."[218] Elliot Cohen's monograph essayed a taxonomy of yellow dog agreements one of which he termed the "open shop" agreement. Illustrative of it was the one used by the Indianapolis Street Railway Company in 1914. It obligated the workers to obey all rules, present and future, that might be made by the company; not to engage in any strike activities; to submit all grievances to arbitration *individually* and without consultation or agreement with other workers or the union. In return, the company agreed to run "an open shop" and not to lock-out or discharge the men "wholly without cause."[219]

That this contract left the worker free to join a union was irrelevant: the evil was the restriction of the individual to individual activity just as Senator Norris argued on the Senate floor.[220]

The inescapable conclusion is that the Court's self-mesmerized view of economic and social theory[221]—previously of freedom of contract, now of bilateral arbitration—has set the law back exactly a hundred years, to *Hitchman Coal & Coke*. It is as if the Norris-LaGuardia Act had never been enacted.

Lest this seem hyperbolic, note the full text of Epic Systems' policy:

> Waiver of Class and Collective Claims. I also agree that covered claims will be arbitrated only on an individual basis, and that both Epic *and I waive the right to* participate in or *receive money or any other relief from any class, collective, or representative proceeding*. No party may bring a claim on behalf of other individuals, and any arbitrator hearing my claim may not: (i) combine more than one individual's claim or claims into a single case; (ii) participate in or facilitate notification of others of potential claims; or (iii) arbitrate any form of a class, collective, or representative proceeding. [Italics added.]

---

217. The U.S. Court of Appeals for the Fifth Circuit sustained the NLRB's holding that employees, apparently not unionized, have a right to display a button supporting an increase in the minimum wage contrary to their employer's dress code policy prohibiting the display of buttons. In-N-Out Burger, Inc. v. NLRB, 894 F.3d 707 (5th Cir. 2018).
218. Seidman, *supra* n. 126.
219. Elliot Cohen, The Yellow Dog Contract 6 (1932) (italics in original, partially excised).
220. See the text accompanying *supra* n. 128.
221. *Supra* n. 43.

In addition to Norris–LaGuardia's "catch-all," the Act sets out nine specific cases of restrictions on a concerted activity which courts were forbidden to enforce, that gave specific direction to what the right to engage in concerted activity for mutual aid or protection was intended to reach. One such provision disallowed the courts the power to enforce contractual restrictions on "Paying or giving to ... any person participating or interested in ... [a] labor dispute, any ... moneys or things of value,"[222] a "labor dispute" being "any controversy concern terms and conditions of employment."[223] As this aspect of Epic Systems' policy passed without judicial notice, it cannot be assumed that the Court's decision would give it effect as well; but, there is no reason, given the Court's rationale—that the FAA trumps the Norris–LaGuardia Act and that arbitration clauses must be enforced as written—why even this provision would not be enforced.

Third, from the practical standpoint, one has to wonder what purpose the preclusion of group claims serves. All these cases before the Court concerned the Fair Labor Standards Act which makes express provisions for the litigation of group claims, which provision can now be obviated by an employer's policy. That provision rests on the proposition that by permitting employees to proceed collectively, the FLSA provides employees the advantages of pooling resources and lowering individual costs so that those with relatively small claims may pursue relief where individual litigation might otherwise be cost-prohibitive. It also yields efficiencies for the judicial system through resolution in one proceeding of common issues arising from the same allegedly wrongful activity affecting numerous individuals.[224]

Preclusion of group resort means that two or more workers who have suffered a common legal wrong are prohibited from challenging that wrong in common. If they are to claim their legal due, they are required to do so only individually. Were that to occur, employers imposing such a prohibition on group challenges would face the prospect of a multiplicity of bilateral arbitrations, each subject separately to discovery of the same documents, depositions of the same managers, presentation of oral testimony on the same practice or decisions made by same people, subject to the same arguments as to events and to the credibility of testimony regarding them, no matter how cumulative or repetitive in the aggregate. This would be the case if each of these aggrieved employees were to pursue a claim. As no employee would be a party to any other employee's action, each would make his or her case afresh. Were a large number who claim to have suffered the same wrong to bring individual arbitrations—all workers of African descent or all women workers who have been denied promotion by an arguably discriminatory test, all older workers disqualified by a novel job requirement that arguably has a discriminatory impact on grounds of age, those of the company's employees allegedly denied donning and doffing or overtime pay—employers would face a procedural morass: line and human resource managers would be required to devote weeks, perhaps months, to repetitive discovery and testimony in as many individual arbitrations as there are claimants.

222. 29 U.S.C. §104(c).
223. 29 U.S.C. §113(c).
224. Halle v. West Penn Allegheny Health Sys., Inc., 842 F.3d 215, 223 (3d Cir. 2016) *citing* Hoffman-La Roche Inc. v. Sperling, 493 U.S. 165, 170 (1989).

As the benefit for efficiency in dispute resolution in allowing collective claims to be brought in a single proceeding is echoed in the reciprocal benefit to employers for the resolution of those claims, why would employers put themselves in a position of potentially facing the procedural morass of a multiplicity of repetitive actions? The obvious answer is that they do not expect those actions ever to be brought. As Horton and Chandrasekher's study points out, though the argument for arbitration is that it makes justice more accessible to workers, the reality is that "few employees accept the invitation."[225] Preclusion of group claims bids fair to avoid any meaningful legal accountability.

Though legality of substituting employer-sponsored arbitration for the courts and the ability of employers to atomize employee-claimants in their arbitration systems is settled, whether the problem has been laid to rest remains to be seen.

225. Horton & Chandrasekher, *supra* n. 213 at 471.

CHAPTER 5

# Labor's Questions at the Century's Turning

As the U.S. edges toward the end of the first quarter of the twenty-first century, labor's problems are a mixture of somethings old, even if in new guise, and somethings new.

## §5.01 SOMETHINGS OLD

### [A] Wages

#### *[1] The Minimum Wage*

Congress set the national minimum wage in 1938 at slightly above "starvation wages." Unlike those countries that index or provide a mechanism for the regular review and updating of the minimum wage, the U.S. sets the federal minimum by legislation. Any change requires Congressional action.

The current federal minimum, $7.25 per hour, was legislated in 2007. Most minimum wage workers work part-time, are women—half are white women—and are evenly divided between those under and over 25. If a minimum wage worker worked full-time, as most do not, the gross annual wage would be $13,195. For a single mother of two, a not uncommon scenario, the poverty line is $17,552. To be a full-time minimum waged worker in America is to live in poverty, it would seem.[226]

226. In contrast, the Australian minimum wage—which the Australians consider a minimum, not a "living wage"—is set annually by the Australian Fair Work Commission with regard to economic consequences and the "relevant living standards and needs of the low paid." Fair Work Act [Australia] §28. The Commission sets the minimum wage as a percentage—a "bite"—on the median adult full-time wage. Today, it is set at just below 54% of the median. This produces a minimum wage of Australian $18.29 per hour. Fair Work Commission Annual Wage Review 2016-2017 ¶32 (2017). Were the U.S. federal minimum to be set at the Australian "bite" of 54% of the median adult wage, a full-time minimum wage worker in the U.S. would earn $23,362 a year.

To be sure, purchasing power may be very different in the two countries. To account for that one could use the "Big Mac" index, that is to determine of how much time a minimum

Some on the political right argue that if one factors in the Earned Income Tax Credit and other forms of assistance for those who qualify—Supplemental Nutrition Assistance Program, rental housing assistance, and Medicaid which provides medical insurance for those in poverty—there is no poverty in America.[227] Granting that public benefits do partially ameliorate conditions for the working poor, some advocates for a higher minimum wage argue that these are costs taxpayers should not bear: that if employers paid higher wages expenditures for public assistance would decline.[228]

The minimum wage is much in the public eye today, with economists making conflicting claims about the consequences of an increase: neo-classical economists attend almost exclusively to the effect of an increase on employment[229]; welfare economists attend to that, but to other consequences as well—reduction in labor turnover and training costs, ripple effects on those paid slightly above the minimum—and tend to endorse a "moderate" increase.[230] Others have paid attention to the elasticity of demand for the product or service; that is, the capacity of employers to pass the wage cost increase on to consumers.[231]

Illustration 3 presents a view of the minimum wage today. It is instructive to compare this to Illustration 2 extolling the enactment of the minimum wage in 1939.

---

wage worker must work in order to be able to purchase an internationally standardized, locally produced consumer good, the McDonalds' "Big Mac," Bureau of Labor Statistics, Household Data Annual Averages Table 3.7 (2018). In Australia, in January 2018, the average cost of a Big Mac was A$5.90. In the U.S., U.S. $5.28. Where the two minimum wage worker stand is set out below:

*Number of Minutes a Minimum Wage Worker Must Work to Purchase a Big Mac*

| *Australia* | *U.S.* |
|---|---|
| 19.34 min | 43.64 min |

227. Jim Tankersley and Margot Sanger-Katz, *Declaring War on Poverty 'Largely Over,' White House Urges Work Requirements for Aid*, N.Y. Times (July 12, 2018). We are not told whether any members of the President's Council of Economic Advisors, which drew this conclusion, includes any single mothers working in minimum wage jobs.
228. Ken Jacobs, Ian Perry, and Jennifer MacGillvary, *The High Public Cost of Low Wages: Poverty-Level Wages Cost U.S. Taxpayers $152.8 Billion Each Year in Public Support for Working Families*, U.C. Berkley Center for Labor Research and Education Research Brief (Apr. 2015).
229. *E.g.* David Newmark & William Wascher, MINIMUM WAGES (2010) and Congressional Budget Office, The Effects of a Minimum Wage Increase on Employment and Family Income (Feb. 2014).
230. *E.g.* Dale Belman & Paul Wolfson, WHAT DOES THE MINIMUM WAGE DO? (2014).
231. In one study of fast food operations in a city in California that increased its minimum wage by 25%, researchers found that fast food stores, in which the lion's share of minimum waged workers were found, increased their prices by 1.45% as a result. Sylvia Allegretto & Michael Reich, *Are Local Minimum Wages Absorbed by Price Increases? Estimates from Internet-Based Restaurant Menus*, 71 ILR Rev. 35 (2018).

**Illustration 3**

Reprinted with permission of the artist.

However, the states and some cities that are free to set their own minimum wage are increasingly doing so—29 states and over forty local governments thus far—some with the goal of a wage more than double the federal minimum.[232]

### *[2] Wage Theft*

"Wage theft" is used to describe an employer's intentional failure to pay an employee all that the worker is legally entitled to. The most common forms of wage theft are:

- **Minimum wage violations:** Paying workers less than the legal minimum wage.
- **Overtime violations:** Failing to pay nonexempt employees time-and-a-half for hours worked in excess of 40 hours per week.
- **Off the clock violations:** Asking employees to work off the clock before or after their shifts.
- **Meal break violations:** Denying workers their legal meal breaks.

232. Economic Policy Institute's Minimum Wage Tracker (online); *see also* Amelia Josephson, *The Cities With the Highest (and Lowest) Real Minimum Wage—2017 Edition* (July 26, 2017). National Employment Law Project, *City Minimum Wage Laws: Recent Trends and Economic Evidence* (Apr. 2016).

- **Pay stub and illegal deductions:** Taking illegal deductions from wages or not distributing pay stubs.
- **Tipped minimum wage violations:** Confiscating tips from workers or failing to pay tipped workers the difference between their tips and the legal minimum wage.
- **Employee misclassification violations:** Misclassifying employees as independent contractors to pay a wage lower than the legal minimum.[233]

In 1933, Carroll Daugherty observed that the "occasional" inability of the worker to collect from his employer the wages actually earned was a problem.[234] The problem is no longer occasional, if it ever was. Given the rise of low-wage service jobs, exacerbated by fissurization and franchising, and the decline of unions which had served to check employer opportunism, wage theft has become an all too common business model for a subset of employers.[235] One study estimates the total annual income exacted by employers by wage violations to come to $15 billion.[236] The question is whether, in the absence of unions, some more effective means of assuring compliance can be found.

The conventional model is that deterrence—and so compliance—is a function of the likelihood of detection times the cost of violation.[237] As the remedies for wage theft are little more than having to pay what the employer should have paid to begin with me, plus attorney fees, and as the victims often know little of their rights or of means of securing redress the law's deterrent effect is small to negligible.

The situation is exacerbated by the U.S. Supreme Court's decision in *Epic Systems* discussed earlier. Prior to it, low-wage workers could bring group actions for all those commonly situated vis-à-vis a violation of federal wage and hour law and could participate in a class action for violation of cognate state laws. But if an employer imposes a mandatory arbitration policy that precludes group claims that road will have been closed. The single employee, perhaps uneducated and vulnerable to retaliation, must find a lawyer to bring her single claim, small in the scale of things, for example, of unpaid overtime effected by a manager's directive to work "off the clock" or by the more sophisticated and less detectable means of having her wages shaved by clever

233. David Cooper & Teresa Kroeger, Employers steal billions from workers' paychecks each year, EPI Report (May 10, 2017) at p. 3.
234. Daugherty, *supra* n. 37.
235. *See e.g.* Marc Doussard, DEGRADED WORK: THE STRUGGLE AT THE BOTTOM OF THE LABOR MARKET 233 (2013).

> With a low ratio of inspectors per establishment and minimal penalties for noncompliance, evading the law is not a covert competitive tactic in service industries—it's a basic, uncontested business practice on public display. The other factors segmenting these labor markets are very important in their own right, but the basic nonenforcement of core laws provides the binding framework for the day-to-day operation of workplaces.

236. Cooper & Kroeger, *supra* n. 233.
237. George Stigler, *The Optimum Enforcement of Laws*, 78 J. Pol. Econ. 526 (1970).

manipulation,[238] in order to bring her claim and hers alone into the company's arbitration system.

It has been argued that the calculus of likelihood of "detection times remedial consequence" could be reset by making the latter more expansive.[239] It has also been suggested that a legal model used in coal mining in the last century could be refurbished to provide a union-like representative presence in the workplace to police wage payment.[240] In the event, the problem of wage and hour law compliance remains a labor problem.

### *[3] Wage Payment*

Wage payment laws of the late nineteenth and early twentieth centuries required workers to be paid promptly and fully in U.S. currency, but, checks or direct bank deposits meet statutory requirements. Payment in cash, common at the company's paymaster's office in the nineteenth century, has disappeared. This leaves wage payment to be made by check or direct bank deposit. However, a large number of Americans, as many as eighty million, have no bank accounts[241]: of those who work, wages cannot be deposited directly, nor checks cashed save at check cashing companies that serve the working poor and that charge significant fees for the service.

Into this gap, banks have offered to provide payroll debit cards to companies. These can save payroll costs for employers, benefit the bank, and be of potential benefit to employees who might otherwise have no choice but to use check cashing companies. A study conducted by the New York State Attorney General found that in 2013, 5.8 million workers were paid via payroll cards, which mode of payment was expected to double in five years.[242] Though benefiting employees in some regards, the N.Y. Attorney General's survey of thirty-eight voluntarily participating companies revealed significant problems: "Virtually all payroll card programs charge fees for card-related activities, and these fees can add up, reducing the meager take-home pay received by the lowest paid workers in the state."[243]

The Federal Reserve Bank has extended the protections of the Electronic Fund Transfer Act[244] to cover payroll accounts for the financial institutions subject to it.[245] In

238. Elizabeth Tippett, Charlotte Alexander & Zev Eigen, *When Timekeeping Software Undermines Compliance*, 19 Yale J.L. & Tech. 1 (2017).
239. *See* Daniel Galvin, *Deterring Wage Theft: Alt-Labor, State Politics, and Policy Determinants of Minimum Wage Compliance*, 14 Perspectives on Politics 324 (2016).
240. Matthew Finkin, *From Weight Checking to Wage Checking: Arming Workers to Combat Wage Theft*, 90 Ind. L.J. 851 (2015).
241. Gosia Glinska, *Fighting Financial Exclusion: How to Serve 88 Million Americans Who Have No Bank*, Forbes (June 5, 2014).
242. Office of N.Y. State Attorney General, Pinched by Plastic: Impact of Payroll Cards on Low-Wage Workers 3 (June 12, 2014).
243. *Id.* at 1. Because the user-employee is subject to a fee, a Pennsylvania court held the mandatory use of a debit card did not comply with that state's wage payment law. Siciliano v. Mueller, 149 A.3d 863 (Pa. Super. 2016) *app. den* 169 A.3d 546 (Penn. 2017).
244. 15 U.S.C. § 1693b.
245. 15 C.F.R. Part 205, § 205.18 (governing "financial institution offering payroll card accounts").

addition, nine states have legislated, thus far, to address some of the harsher aspects of debit card wage payment.[246] The means of wage payment remains a labor problem.

### [B] The Precarity of Work and Hours

The precarity of work as a product of labor segmentation—the resort to part-time, on-call, leased workers, and independent contractors—has been discussed as posing a bundle of labor problems to which extant solutions, grounded in the labor model of the mid-twentieth century, do not adequately respond. The failure of the systems of unemployment compensation, for example, has been studied in depth.[247] But the particular feature that has drawn most attention is the precarity of work hours.

The hours of work has been a contentious issue since the early nineteenth century. The struggle then was about excessive hours. Workers demanded first the ten and, later, the eight hour day. Today, computer software has enabled employers to predict their need for workers, especially service workers, on short notice in "real time" on the basis of customer flow and to schedule workers according to the computer's estimate.[248] This has become a labor problem as the precarity of hours affects the predictability and stability of work, income, and even mental health[249]: employees subject to sudden schedule change cannot plan for such things as child care, medical visits, and even for their work in other jobs. To circle back, the particular unresponsiveness of unemployment compensation to the precarity of hours has been dealt with separately and it's worth noticing again, especially that employees who leave their jobs because of volatile scheduling practices are seen as not having "good cause" for quitting if such schedules are deemed customary in the industry or occupation, or if the employer disclosed to the employee at the time of hiring that such scheduling practices were prevalent.[250]

---

246. The provisions are canvassed in *Payroll Cards and the States: Benefits, Challenges, and Action*, National Association of Attorneys General, 8 NAA Gazette Archive No. 9 (2018). This does not include New York whose action was taken administratively which was set aside on administrative appeal. In Re Global Cash Card, Inc., N.Y.S. Industrial Board of Appeals, Doc. No. PR 16-1205 (Feb. 16, 2017) and is now under judicial review. *In the Application of Reardon*, N.Y. Sup. Ct. No. 02643-17 (Apr. 17, 2017). A Pennsylvania court held payment by debit card to violate that state's wage payment law. Siciliano v. Mueller, 149 A.3d 863 (Pa. Super. 2016).
247. Rachel West et al., Strengthening Unemployment Protections in America: Modernizing Unemployment Insurance and Establishing a Jobseeker's Allowance (June 2016) (Report of the Center for American Progress and others).
248. Françoise Carré & Chris Tilly, Where Bad Jobs Are Better: Retail Jobs Across Counties and Companies 123 (2017).
249. Lonnie Golden, Irregular Work Scheduling and Its Consequences (EPI Briefing Paper) (Apr. 9, 2015). Susan Lambert, Peter Fugiel & Julia Henry, Precarious Work Scheduling among Early-Career Employees in the U.S.: A National Snapshot (EINet report) (Aug. 27, 2014). Center for Law & Social Policy, Retail Action Project, and Women Employment, Tackling Unstable and Unpredictable Work Schedules: A Policy Brief on Guaranteed Minimum Hours and Reporting Pay Policies (n.d.).
250. Liz Ben-Ishal, Rick McHugh & Claire McKenna, Out of Sync: The Unemployment Insurance Rules Fail Workers with Volatile Job Schedule, National Employment Law Project (Aug. 2015).

Two legal approaches have been taken to deal with the problem. One is to require notice of work scheduling and of changes in it, as in Germany, for example.[251] San Francisco requires that workers be given two weeks' notice of their work schedules.[252] The other is to require that an employee who reports for duty is to be paid for a set amount of hours of work when that work is not required. These provisions echo "call-in pay" obligations commonly contained in collective bargaining agreements. Thus far, where this route has been taken they vary from one hour,[253] two hours,[254] three hours,[255] to at most, four.[256]

### [C] Paid Leave

As far as the Congress has been prepared to go in terms of reconciling family life and work life is to mandate a maximum twelve-week period of unpaid leave for the employee to attend to personal or family medical needs. In keeping with the role of state and local government as innovators in labor protection, at least nine states and two dozen cities have legislated to require paid family leave.[257]

### [D] Wrongful Dismissal

The effort of the National Conference of Uniform State Laws in 1991 to draw attention to the issue of wrongful dismissal—wrongful not because of statutory retaliation or violation of public policy, wrongful because arbitrary, ill-informed, excessive, or even devious[258]—and to offer a means of legal redress failed. The issue has become dormant.

This presents the question of why the U.S., unlike most of the developed world, has no general law of fair or wrongful dismissal: why the issue has so little contemporary purchase. One answer is that American society values contractual freedom. Placed in comparative perspective, this means that unlike workers in all these countries, common law and civil law, European, Asian, and South American, workers in the U.S. either *want* their employers to have the power to dismiss them at-will or do not want the law to interfere in dismissal decisions, do not want their employment relationships to become juridified.

---

251. Bernd Waas, *Germany* in MULTINATIONAL HUMAN RESOURCE MANAGEMENT AND THE LAW 129 (Matthew Finkin & Joel Cutcher-Gershenfeld eds., 2013).
252. San Francisco Police Code, Art. 33G, Sec. 3300G.2.
253. N.J. Rev. Stat. § 12:56-5.5.
254. N.H. Laws §275:43-a.
255. 455 CMR §2.03 [Mass.] (for employees scheduled to work three or more hours); R.I. Gen Laws §28-12-3.2.
256. Conn. Lab. Dept. Reb. §31-62-D2(d) (only for workers in "mercantile trade"); 12 NYCRR §142-2.3 [New York].
257. 27 DLR 22 (Feb. 8, 2018); 9 DLR 32 (Jan. 12, 2018); 452 DLR 23 (Dec. 22, 2017).
258. In Wisehart v. Meganck, 66 P.3d 124 (Colo. App. 2002), for example, the at-will rule was held to insulate the fabrication of a false ground of discharge; as the job was held at-will, as the employee could be fired for any or no reason, it was irrelevant that the discharge was based on a fabricated reason.

This assertion has been made by libertarians and Manchesterian economists. One of the former, Richard Epstein, asserts that "the contract at will is *sought* by *both* persons."[259] One of the latter, Andrew Morriss, asserts that the at-will rule "is an allocation of decisionmaking authority between the public and private sectors which serves the needs of both employers *and employees*."[260] As the rule so obviously serves employee *needs*, they would surely want to have it so, just as Epstein says.

These claims are counter-intuitive. If they are correct, then America would truly be exceptional. On closer examination, however, three reasons emerge to be skeptical of the claim.

First, job security is most often a "public good." A single, non-indispensable worker who insists on it as a condition of her employment is most unlikely to be hired: a commitment to just cause in discharge for her would advantage her over all her otherwise similarly situated (or fungible) co-workers and would be most unlikely to be agreed to, as fomenting division in the workplace; indeed, the very asking of it might send a signal disqualifying her for further consideration. Thus she, lacking the power to bargain a condition common to all, and lacking the power to secure it for herself, would be most unlikely to raise it at all, to risk just that signaling effect. In fact, were she to be an incumbent worker and were she to ask that the employer commit not to dismiss her except for just cause, under the at-will rule she can be discharged for having asked.[261] This explains why a near universal feature of collective bargaining agreements in the U.S. is to require just cause to dismiss: the union is positioned to bargain for the group over a condition of work that affects them all; the individual worker is not.

Second, the exceptionalism argument assumes that workers know that they can be fired at any time for no reason and, knowing that that is so, they desire to have it so. There is rather little empirical evidence of what employees know of the law, but one well-crafted study, albeit only of one city and county in one state, concluded that there is a "striking level of misunderstanding" of basic legal rules governing employment and that workers tend systematically to overestimate their legal protection.[262] American workers seem to think that if something is wrong, is very wrong—say, the dismissal of a long-serving worker for no reason whatsoever—it must surely be unlawful.

Third, legislative change requires either an effective interest group pressing for it, public outrage over the issue, or both. In terms of interest group representation, fair dismissal law is not high on the agenda for organized labor. Some in the leadership are suspicious of a measure that, if successful, might enervate the demand for union

259. Richard Epstein, *In Defense of the Contract At Will*, 51 U. Chi. L. Rev. 947, 954 (1984) (emphases added).

260. Andrew Morriss, *Bad Data, Bad Economics, Bad Policy: Time to Fire Wrongful Discharge Law*, 74 Tex. L. Rev. 1901, 1902 (1966) (emphasis added).

261. Because her demand is individual and not on behalf of a group, it would not be protected by federal labor law. There is law to just this effect concerning wage demands. National Wax Company v. Stephany, 251 NLRB 1064 (1980); Parker Laboratories Inc., 267 NLRB 1174 (1983); Allied Erecting and Dismantling Company Inc., 270 NLRB 277 (1984).

262. Pauline Kim, *Bargaining with Imperfect Information: A Study of Worker Perceptions of Legal Protection in an At-Will World*, 83 Cornell L. Rev. 105, 133 (1997).

representation and collective bargaining; that fair dismissal comes with union representation and only union representation. The trial bar, which donates considerable amounts to political campaigns, opposed fair dismissal law; it would reduce attorney fees available from workplace tort litigation.[263] In sum, the interests of unrepresented workers are not likely to be legislatively represented directly or by proxy.

One way to test the Libertarian-Manchesterian claim would be to put it to a vote; and such a natural experiment was nearly run, in Colorado in 2008. Jonathan Coors, a reactionary scion of a brewing dynasty, was able to place on the ballot an amendment to the state constitution that would have Colorado become a "right to work" state, making it unlawful for unions to agree with employers to require nonmembers who are represented by the union to pay to the union a fair share of the cost of their being represented. In response, unions mounted an effort to place a referendum on the ballot to abrogate the at-will rule, to require employers in Colorado to prove just cause to discharge employees. "In an alliance born in part in fear," corporate executives pledged $3 million to defeat the Coors amendment if labor would withdraw the ballot measure.[264] The unions agreed. The ballot abolishing the at-will rule was withdrawn. The money was paid. The anti-Coors campaign was launched. The Coors amendment failed. As a result, the natural experiment of an electoral test of American exceptionalism was never run.

Even so, it is instructive that Coloradan business was willing to bet a considerable sum on the belief that American workers do not differ from their counterparts around the globe: that once a strenuous campaign was joined, as it surely would have been—the unions had raised $11 for their ballot initiative—once, that is, workers became fully educated about, or drenched in the facts of the legal regime that governed them, they would vote to change it.

### [E] Mobility

The policy of the law since the Gilded Age has been to support worker mobility. Wage payment law and even the at-will rule buttressed the ability of the worker to quit: to take her abilities and skills elsewhere; to better herself. In recent years, however, employers have launched devices to retain employees by restraining their ability to take their skills elsewhere, to get better jobs. In addition, a little-noticed aspect of public law affecting mobility—occupational licensure—heretofore dormant has begun to draw attention.

#### *[1] Contractual Restraints on Mobility*

At common law, an employee could agree with an employer not to take a job with a competitor after leaving the employer—but only for certain kinds of work, for a limited

263. Theodore J. St. Antoine, *The Model Employment Termination Act: A Fair Compromise*, 356 Annals of the American Academy of Political and Social Science 93, 101 (1994).
264. Stephanie Simon, *Executives Pledge Funds as Unions Drop Colorado Initiatives*, Wall St. Journal (Oct. 3, 2008); Editorial, *Colorado's Labor Showdown*, Wall St. Journal (Oct. 4, 2008).

period of time and within a bounded geographic area of competition—if the agreement was grounded in an interest other than the employer's desire to be free of competition, in the archetypical case, to protect a trade secret.[265] It would be the case that employees most likely to be subject to such an agreement would be in a strategic situation vis-à-vis the employer as the possessor of secret or sensitive confidential business information. When a franchisor's contract with a franchisee who was, in fact, only an individual person working for himself doing automobile trim repair, contained a covenant not to compete the Texas Supreme Court disallowed enforcement: it stressed the public interest in having the individual able to exercise his skills and talents and concluded that an agreement prohibiting the person "from engaging in a common calling" could not be enforced.[266] The sentiment was not shared by the Texas legislature which quickly repealed the distinction.[267]

In recent years, employers of persons in such common callings—office support, installation and repair, personal care and services, and even fast food preparation—have required these employees to execute restrictive covenants. Exemplar Three sets out the text of an agreement a large fast food franchise required its franchisees to have their employees sign as a condition of employment. The name of the company has been changed. All else is as the company required.

**Exemplar Three**

**EMPLOYEE CONFIDENTIALITY AND NON-COMPETITION AGREEMENT**

THIS CONFIDENTIALITY AND NON-COMPETITION AGREEMENT (the "Agreement") is made as of __________, _____ (the "Effective Date") (regardless of the dates of the parties' signature) by and between a(n) ________________ ("Employer"), and ________________ ("Employee).

1. **Background**. Employer operates as a franchisee of Delphie's Deli Franchise, LLC, a Delaware limited liability company ("DDF"). DDF franchisees DELPHIE'S DELI® Sandwich Shops operating at various locations throughout the country and, in connection with those activities, has invested (and continues to invest) substantial time, effort, and money in developing the products sold to customers of DELPHIE'S DELI® Sandwich Shops and refining the procedures to be used in operating DELPHIE'S DELI® Sandwich Shops, all of which DDF considers to be "Confidential Information," as further defined in this Agreement. Employer, as a franchisee of DDF, entered into that certain franchise agreement dated __________, ____ with DDF or its predecessor in interest Delphie's Deli Franchise Inc. (the "Franchise Agreement"). Pursuant to the Franchise Agreement, Employer uses the Confidential Information in its operation of the franchise(s) located at __________________. Pursuant to the

265. *See, generally*, Harlan Blake, *Employee Agreements Not to Compete*, 73 Harv. L. Rev. 625 (1960).
266. Hill v. Mobile Auto Trim, Inc., 725 S.W.2d 168, 172 (Tex. 1987).
267. Tex. Bus. & Com. Code § 15.50 (1989).

Franchise Agreement, all employees of Employer having access to the Confidential Information are required to execute this Agreement.

Employee desires to become an employee of Employer and acknowledges that, during the term of his or her employment with Employer, he or she will have access to Confidential Information in order to perform his or her employee duties. Employee understands the importance of Confidential Information to Employer and DDF and of preserving the confidentiality of Confidential Information. Employer is willing to hire Employee only on the condition that Employee agrees to comply with this Agreement's obligations. Employee understands that complying with this Agreement is essential to protect Employer's and DDF's legitimate business interests.

2. **Confidentiality**. (a) The term "Confidential Information," as used in this Agreement, means certain confidential and proprietary information, including trade secrets, relating to the development and operation of DELPHIE'S DELI® Sandwich Shops. Confidential information further includes, but is not limited to: (a) plans and specifications for developing DELPHIE'S DELI® Sandwich Shops. (b) training methods, materials, programs, and systems for employees of DELPHIE'S DELI® Sandwich Shops; (c) methods, techniques, menus, recipes, formats, specifications, standards, systems, procedures, sales and marketing techniques, and knowledge and experience in developing and operating DELPHIE'S DELI® Sandwich Shops; (d) marketing, advertising, and promotional programs for DELPHIE'S DELI® Sandwich Shops and the DELPHIE'S DELI® System; (e) Operations Manuals; (f) knowledge of specifications for and suppliers of ingredients, products, materials, supplies, equipment, and services used in connection with developing and operating DELPHIE'S DELI® Sandwich Shops; (g) the identities of suppliers and the terms of supplier contracts; (h) knowledge of operating results and financial performance of DELPHIE'S DELI® Sandwich Shops; (i) ongoing product and service research and development; and (j) new site investigation or selection criteria.

   (b) In consideration of Employer's willingness to employ Employee, the Compensation that Employer will pay to Employee, the training that Employer will provide to Employee, and the introduction of Employee to Employer's customers and suppliers, Employee agrees to use the Confidential Information only to the extent reasonably necessary to perform his or her duties on behalf of the Employer, taking into consideration the confidential nature of the Confidential Information. Employee acknowledges and agrees that neither Employee nor any other person or entity will acquire any interest in or right to use the Confidential Information other than in performing his or her duties during the scope of his or her employment by Employer and that any unauthorized use or duplication of the Confidential Information would be detrimental to Employer and DDF, would damage Employer's and DDF's legitimate business interests, and would constitute a breach of Employee's obligations of confidentiality and would further constitute an unfair method of competition with Employer and DDF and/or franchised or company-owned DELPHIE'S DELI® Sandwich Shops.

(c) Employee acknowledges and agrees that the Confidential Information is confidential to and a valuable asset of Employer and DDF. The Confidential Information will be disclosed to Employee solely on the condition that Employee agrees, and Employee therefore does hereby agree that, during and after his or her employment by Employer, he or she: (a) will not use the Confidential Information in any other business or capacity; (b) will maintain the absolute confidentiality of each item of Confidential Information for as long as such item remains confidential; (c) will not make unauthorized copies of any portion of the Confidential Information disclosed in written or any other tangible form; and (d) will adopt and implement all reasonable procedures prescribed from time to time by Employer and DDF to prevent unauthorized use or disclosure of or access to the Confidential Information, including any such procedures implemented following the execution of this Agreement.

(d) Employee acknowledges and agrees that DDF will own any developments in the operation of a DELPHIE'S DELI® Sandwich Shop or concerning its products that Employee might create during his or her employment by Employer.

3. **Non-Competition Covenant.** Employee covenants and agrees that, during his or her employment with Employer and for a period of two (2) years after either the effective date of termination of his or her employment for any reason, whether voluntary or involuntary and whether by Employer or Employee, or the date on which Employee begins to comply with this paragraph, whichever is later, he or she will not have any direct or indirect interest in or perform services for (whether as an owner, partner, investor, director, officer, representative, manager, employee, principal, agent, advisor, or consultant) any business which derives more than ten percent (10%) of its revenue from selling submarine, hero-type, deli-style, pita and or wrapped or rolled sandwiches and which is located within three (3) miles of either (1) [insert address of employment], or (2) any such other DELPHIE'S DELI® Sandwich Shop operated by DDF, one of its authorized franchisees, or any of DDF's affiliates.

Employee also acknowledges and agrees that, for at least twelve (12) months after the effective date of termination of his or her employment for any reason, whether voluntary or involuntary and whether by Employer or Employee, Employee may not become a partner of or investor/owner with, or work for, another DELPHIE'S DELI® Sandwich Shop franchisee. Employee acknowledges that other DELPHIE'S DELI® Sandwich Shop franchisees are contractually prohibited by DDF from recruiting Employee as a partner or investor/owner, or from hiring Employee, for at least twelve (12) months after Employee leaves his or her employment with Employer (regardless of the reason for his or her departure).

4. **Solicitation.** Employee agrees to disclose to Employer immediately upon receipt any employment offers made by any competitor of Employer (as defined in Section 3 above).
5. **Amendment.** This Agreement may be modified only in a writing signed by Employer and Employee.
6. **Costs and Attorneys' Fees.** Employee agrees to reimburse Employer and DDF for all costs and expenses, including attorneys' fees, that Employer or DDF incur to enforce this Agreement against Employee.
7. **Governing Law.** This Agreement and the relationship of the parties will be governed by the laws of the State of __________, without regard to its conflicts of laws rules.
8. **Severability.** The parties desire that this Agreement be enforced to the fullest extent possible under applicable law and therefore agree that, if any provision is deemed to be unenforceable or unlawful, that provision will be ignored to the extent of its unenforceability or unlawfulness, but the remaining portions of that provision, and this Agreement as a whole, will be enforced to the fullest extent possible. The parties expressly agree that any court may "blue pencil" any provision in this agreement and enforce it to the maximum extent allowed under applicable law.
9. **Third Party Beneficiary.** Employee recognizes that the parties intended for DDF to be a third party beneficiary of this Agreement and that DDF at its election may enforce this Agreement with or without the authorization or cooperation of Employer. Employee understands that any action by Employee in violation of this Agreement will cause DDF irreparable harm and Employee therefore acknowledges that DDF may apply for an injunction preventing Employee from violating this Agreement and Employee agrees to pay DDF's costs and attorneys' fees incurred by DDF to enforce this Agreement as provided in Section 6 above.

**EMPLOYER**

Signature: __________________
Name (print): __________________
Title: __________________
Date: __________________

**EMPLOYEE**

Signature: __________________
Name (print): __________________
Title: __________________

Note that the agreement designates large bodies of information as constituting trade secrets or protected confidential business information. This would supply an interest to support a covenant not to compete *if* the designation were sound. The material so designated falls into three categories: (1) financial information and business plans to which access would be expected to be restricted, that is known only to a small number of managerial employees and which would not be known to the workforce as a whole or to the general public and which could give competitors a competitive advantage; (2) training materials and methods which would be known by all employees the secret or confidential nature of which remains to be seen; and (3) matter that would be known by employees and easily ascertained by any customer—menus, ingredients, even recipes for sandwiches by one who merely opens her sandwich for inspection. Under section 2(b) of the agreement, the disclosure of any of that information, if not "reasonably necessary" to the performance of the employees' duties, would be a breach of contract. Moreover, the employee is required to "maintain the *absolute* confidentiality of *each* item" listed, and if the Company sues to enforce that provision, the employee would be contractually bound to pay the Company's attorney fees. In other words, if a sandwich delivery person who had signed this agreement tells his girlfriend what is in the sandwich he has just given her, he could be sued for breach of confidentiality and could be required to pay for the employer's costs of the suit even if the employee wins.

More important for purposes here is the covenant not to compete which the disclosure or use of the contractually designated confidential information is supposed to support. The employee—let us take our sandwich maker or delivery man or woman—may not work for another of the franchisor's franchisees for a year and may not work ("perform services") in *any* capacity for *any* business that derives as little as 10% of its income from selling sandwiches within three miles of this location for two years.

Turning first to the restriction on mobility within the franchise network, the agreement not to work for another of the franchisor's franchisees anywhere for a one year period adds nothing to the franchisees' commitment to the franchisor not to hire employees of other franchisees. No contract with employees is necessary for franchisors to include "no poaching" provisions in their franchise contracts: nothing is gained, legally, in making an employee aware of the prohibition. It functions simply as an *in terrorem* device to deter employees from applying elsewhere. In fact, some franchisors have imposed "no poaching" provisions on their franchisees, forbidding them from hiring employees from other units in the same franchised network.[268] Nor franchises alone. Similar "no poach" agreements have been made, most prominently in the health care and the high-tech industry where the competition for talent can be intense. In 2016, the U.S. Department of Justice and the Federal Trade Commission warned that no poaching agreements among employers, whether entered into directly or through a third-party intermediary, are per se illegal under the antitrust laws. That means that if the agreement is separate from or not reasonably necessary to a larger

268. Alan Krueger & Orley Ashenfelter, Theory and Evidence on Employer Collusion in the Franchise Sector, Princeton U. Indus. Rel. Section Working Paper No. 614 (Sept. 28, 2017). Anti-poaching pacts have drawn press attention. Conor Dougherty, *Battles Simmer a Workers Try to o to Rivals*, N.Y. Times (July 15, 2017) at A-1; Rachel Abrams, *Trapped in Fast Food's Slow Lane*, N.Y. Times (Sept. 28, 2017) at B-1.

legitimate collaboration between the employers, the agreement is deemed illegal without any inquiry into its competitive effects and that the Department intended to proceed criminally against them.[269]

Turning next to the covenant not to compete, it is difficult to conceive that it would be enforceable in any American state; in fact, the generator of this instrument was sued and agreed to withdraw it, apparently nationwide. But, as one economic study has shown, the point of requiring employees to sign them is not to secure enforcement: as these relatively unsophisticated employees are unlikely to know that these provisions are legally worthless, it is enough that they fear enforcement. These provisions function *in terrorem*. By using them employers reduce the costs of labor turnover.[270] In response, a number of states have or are considering limiting the use of these restrictions.[271] Illinois, for example, prohibits employers from making such agreements with "low-wage employees," defined as persons making $13/hour or the minimum wage whoever is greater.[272]

### *[2] Occupational Licensure*

A time-honored means of restricting competition in the labor market—occupational mobility within a state as well as occupational movement into a state—is to require the practitioner of the profession or trade to secure a license in order to practice it. Commonly, this is conditioned on the satisfactory completion of a prescribed course of study and passage of an examination. These have been termed "fence-me-in" laws.

Historically, the requirement of a license, as a restraint on individual liberty, needs be grounded in some rational relationship to public health, safety, or welfare which the courts would assure.[273] Today, the courts give considerable deference to the legislative judgment that such a connection exists[274] and there been a growing resort to occupational licensure. According to U.S. Census Bureau data, in 1950 the national average was that one in twenty jobs required a license. Today, 20% of the workforce

269. U.S. Dept. of Justice and Federal Trade Commission, Antitrust Guidance for Human Resource Professionals 3 (Oct. 2016). In 2018 anti-trust suit against Apple, Google and other Silicon Valley tech companies were settled for several millions of dollars. 53 DLR (BNA) (Mar. 19, 2018).
270. J.J. Prescott, Norman Bishara & Evan Starr, *Understanding Noncompetition Agreements: The 2014 Noncompete Survey Project*, 2016 Mich. St. L. Rev. 369 (2016). *See also* U.S. Dept. of Treasury Office of Economic Policy, Non-compete Contracts: Economic Effects and Policy Implications (Mar. 2016).
271. Jonathan Shapiro, *Which States Are Likely to Enact Laws Restricting Non-Compete Agreements in 2017?*, The National Law Journal (May 19, 2017).
272. 820 ILCS 90/1.
273. Doctoring, lawyering, and plumbing passed judicial muster; but horseshoeing did not, and emphatically so. Bessette v. People, 62 N.E. 215 (Ill. 1901); In Re Aubry, 78 Pac. 900 (Wash. 1904); People v. Beattie, 89 N.Y.S. 193 (App. Div. 1904) (rejecting the argument that licensure was necessary to protect against animal cruelty.)
274. *E.g.* Sensational Smiles, LLC v. Mullen, 793 F.3d 281 (2d Cir. 2015).

is in licensed occupations.[275] Though long dormant, occupational licensure as a barrier to labor market mobility shows a glimmer of gaining public traction.[276]

### [F] Employee Representation

Market participation became a necessary condition of economic citizenship; necessary, but not sufficient. The sufficient condition was that workers should be able to "participate in some organic way in every decision that affects their welfare," as Woodrow Wilson put it a century ago. In the 30s, that *was* the Labor Question. The answer fashioned at the time was to provide the legal scaffolding for collective bargaining; and, for some decades, it worked. It works no more: private sector union density is below 7%, well below the level of employee representation before collective bargaining became legally protected. Yet employees still desire to have and to exercise a right meaningfully to be heard by their employers on a range of matters of intense concern to them in which they have no other way provided by law to be heard.[277] Indeed, the contest in the public sphere over unionization is no less intense today than during the Gilded Age. From 2006 to 2015, the two organizations most aggressive in seeking "right to work" legislation, the National Right to Work Committee and the National Right to Work Legal Defense Foundation, received contributions totaling $105 million and $64.4 million respectively.[278] Illustration 4 is an anti-union cartoon of 1992.

275. *See generally* Morris Kleiner, Licensing Occupations: Ensuring Quality or Restricting Competition? 1 (2006).
276. Janna Johnson & Morris Kleiner, *Is Occupational Licensing a Barrier to Interstate Migration?*, NBER Working Paper No. 24107 (Dec. 2017); Gayle Cinquegrani, *State Licensing Creates Job Barriers*, Bloomberg Law (Aug. 24, 2018) at p. 1. *See also* The Economic Innovation Group, *The 2017 Distressed Communities Index* 49 (2017) (pointing to "onerous occupational licensure requirements at the local level" as a barrier to community development); H.R. 2155, 115th Cong., 1st sess. (Apr. 26, 2017) (calling for interagency consultation for *intern alia* the "elimination of licenses or certification which pose an unnecessary barrier for entry for aspiring workers.").
277. Thomas Kochan and his colleagues took up afresh the question investigated a generation earlier by Richard Freeman & Joel Rogers, What Workers Want (1999). Kochan and his group also found a significant gap in what workers want to have a say about, what they want to influence, and the extent to which they actually had a say or influence. Thomas Kochan, William Kimball, Duranji Yand & Erin Kelly, Worker Voice in America: A Current Assessment and Exploration of Options, MIT Inst. for Work and Employment Research Working Paper (Jan. 17, 2018). The Freeman and Rogers survey indicated that about a third of non-union workers said they would vote for a union. In the 2017 survey, 46% said they would vote for a union. As Richard Freeman put it earlier, "If unionism were a normal good or service, some smart organization or entrepreneur would step forward and find ways to meet the unfilled demand." Richard Freeman, America Works: Critical Thoughts on the Exceptional U.S. Labor Market 92 (2007).
278. 192 DLR (2017) at p. 9.

**Illustration 4**

Reprinted with permission of the National Right to Work Committee. It is instructive to compare it with Illustration 1, an anti-union cartoon of the Gilded Age. In 1935, compulsory union membership—the "closed shop"—was made unlawful. In 1959, unions were required to adhere to democratic principles for member free speech and in the election of union officers. Does the symbolism of the "Union Boss" today retain the power the "walking delegate" did a century ago? On August 7, 2018, a ballot proposition allowing unions to negotiate for the payment of mandatory fees by nonmembers they represent, an anti-"right to work" law, passed in Missouri by a two-to-one margin.

There seems to be a consensus among scholars who have studied the matter and who are sympathetic to the exercise of employee voice that at least some of the explanation for the decline in union representation—the only systematic mode of collective voice U.S. law allows—lies at the feet of the Labor Act.[279] Consequently, one avenue for address lies in its reformation: significantly strengthening the remedies for violation, that is of more meaningful individual redress for unfair labor practices and the imposition of contract terms resisted by employers in bad faith; better enabling the General Counsel to seek injunctions against employers after the office has filed serious

279. The literature is rich. Among the more notable are Paul Weiler, GOVERNING THE WORKPLACE (1990); Stephen Befort & John Budd, INVISIBLE HANDS, INVISIBLE OBJECTIVES (2009); Cynthia Estlund, *Ossification of American Labor Law*, 102 Colum. L. Rev. 1527 (2002); Kenneth Dau-Schmidt, *Promoting Voice in the American Economy: A Call for Comparative Reform*, 94 Marquette L. Rev. 765 (2011).

unfair labor practice complaints; abolishing the ability of the states to deny the availability of agency fee agreements with unions, so-called right to work laws, permitted by the Taft-Hartley Act; forbidding the permanent replacement of economic strikers; abandoning or loosening restrictions on secondary boycotts; expanding coverage to include those excluded as independent contractors and supervisors; facilitating the inclusion of those up the contracting, franchising, or supply chain to be within the scope of Labor Act obligations to the employees down the contractual chain; expanding the scope of mandatory bargaining issues; requiring the arbitration of the terms of bargaining agreements in the event of impasse in new bargaining relationships; making pre-hire agreements, currently are available only in the construction trades, available in all employments better to provide representation to these in other casual or "gig" work; requiring union recognition whenever the union has secured and has objectively manifested majority support; or, more radically, doing away with exclusive majority representation, perhaps instituting mandatory works councils akin to the German model—and a good deal more.

The problem is not the want of legal imagination; it is the want of political will. The Labor Act has proven intractable of any really serious reform since 1947. That legislative incapacity gives no hint of surcease. Consequently, attention turns to the states and cities which, as we have seen, have become engines of legal change in response to resurging and emerging labor problems. That road is less open here because state or local measures that intrude into matters reserved by the Labor Act to federal action may be precluded—"preempted" is the doctrinal term—by federal law. Thus, state or local efforts to enforce alternative schemes for worker representation will have to face inevitable challenge on preemption grounds.[280] Interestingly, the Labor Act does not address the scope of preemption in terms. Thus the reach and contours of employee representation preemption lie entirely in the hands of the Supreme Court. Given its current composition, it is unlikely that the Court would be amenable to allowing the states greater leeway to facilitate employee representation.

The situation is ironic: that a 1935 federal law intended to establish democratic conditions in industry by sweeping away state laws inimical to its purposes has become—or, in the hands of the Supreme Court, is most likely to be—an insuperable obstacle to local measures conducive to and potentially more effective in realizing that very end. Should that be the case, the only avenue for the realization of economic democracy would require amendment to a law that has proven incapable of significant reform for nearly three quarters of a century. It appears that *the* "Labor Question" of the Gilded Age has resurged, this time without any prospect of successful address.

280. The City of Seattle adopted an ordinance providing for "for-hire vehicle drivers" to engage in collective bargaining *if* they were independent contractors. Inasmuch as the Labor Act does not apply to independent contractors the ordinance was not preempted by it, though it could still face anti-trust attack. Chamber of Commerce v. City of Seattle, 890 F.3d 769 (9th Cir. 2018).

## §5.02 SOMETHINGS NEW

Two questions have emerged as the product of technologies not in existence and barely imagined a half century ago. The first is a cluster of questions that attend the prospect of more and more jobs, and so job-holders, being in electronically mediated "gig" or "on-demand" work. The second centers on the capacity of the state to protect worker privacy in a wired world.

### [A] On-Demand Work[281]

"Gig," "crowd," or "on-demand" work has been declaimed a new institution generating new labor questions which call for the fashioning of new law attuned to these new modes of work.[282] However, the salience of the issues presented depends on the extent to which people will be engaged in gig work as a major source of income and the extent to which this mode of work will become a significant component of the labor market. This question is without a definitive answer thus far and does not want in skepticism.[283]

Even so, the claim of novelty remains to be seen. As this lecture noted at the outset, work has long been "put out," not only to individual contractors but also through complex networks, webs of subcontracting sometimes with the same actors playing different roles at different times or simultaneously.[284] Such was the structure of wool production in Renaissance Florence,[285] of contracting in furniture manufacture in eighteenth-century France, which has been likened to an "oriental bazaar,"[286] and contracting for the home manufacture of garments in Philadelphia of the 1910s, termed a "labyrinthine system."[287]

281. A collection discussing the various forms that "gig" or crowdsourced work takes was edited by Valerio DeStefano and appeared in the Symposium, *Crowdsourcing, the Gig-Economy, and the Law*, 37 Comp. Lab. L. & Pol'y J. No. 3 (2016).
282. *See, e.g.*, Seth Harris & Alan Krueger, *A Proposal for Modernizing Labor Laws for Twenty-First-Century Work: The "Independent Worker,"* 5 (The Hamilton Project Discussion Paper 2015-10, Dec. 2015) ("New and emerging work relationship on the 'online gig economy' do not fit the legal definitions of 'employee' and 'independent contractor' status.")
283. It has been estimated that less than 1% of the U.S. workforce currently is engaged in gig work. E. Brynjolfsson & K. McElheren, *The Rapid Adoption of Data-Driven Decision Making*, 106 Am. Econ. Rev. 133 (2016).
284. *See generally*, Matthew Finkin, *Beclouded Work, Beclouded Workers in Historical Perspective*, 37 Comp. Lab. L. & Pol'y J. 603 (2016).
285. Richard Goldthwaite, THE ECONOMY OF RENAISSANCE FLORENCE 329 (2009).
286. Michael Sonenscher, WORK AND WAGES: NATURAL LAW, POLITICS AND THE EIGHTEENTH CENTURY FRENCH TRADES 23 (1989) (reference omitted) ("Both the form of the wage and the character of the work were typical of a world of short-term arrangements, fleeting opportunities and brief associations, a world which has more in common with a North African or Oriental bazaar (not to mention the neo-classical economists' concept of a spot market) than with the corporate world of eighteenth-century French artisans.").
287. Walter Licht, GETTING WORK: PHILADELPHIA, 1840-1950, 247 (1992) (references omitted):

> A study conducted on domestic industry in the 1910s revealed that manufacturers left the recruitment of home workers entirely in the hands of contractors and they themselves, as one testified, "[had] no means of knowing how many people our

Nevertheless, legal issues do cluster about the organization of work and workers by enterprises via electronic means, directly or through electronic intermediation. These center on two questions: (1) are those engaged in the work "employees" for the purpose of statutes fashioned with more traditional work settings in mind—collective bargaining, minimum wage, wage payment and overtime, antidiscrimination, unemployment compensation, social security, family leave, perhaps occupational health and safety; and, if they are employees, (2) who is, or are, the responsible "employer" or "employers"? A third question follows if the answer to the first is "no"; that is, what rights ought these workers have and against whom?[288]

The reason these questions seem novel and challenging is because the labor law of the twentieth century was developed in response to the regnant model of full-time workers engaged pretty much for the whole of their working lives by a single, large, integrated enterprise.[289] In some cases, the Labor Act is the prime example, the definition of a statutory "employee" was borrowed from the law apportioning liability for tort injury to third parties. This is ill suited to govern the status of an on-demand worker.

On the question of defining the entity or entities responsible for what the law demands, the law of child labor might provide an historical precedent worthy of consideration, as might the nineteenth century's more detailed treatment of responsibility in the chain of railroad construction subcontracting as well.[290] There are precedents at hand.

---

contractors employ[ed]." Even the contractors did not keep close tabs. One agent described his operations as follows: "I go out on Christian Street and pick up a couple of Italian women that know how to finish trousers." The agent reported that he never learned their names, nor how they went about finding and organizing relatives, friends, and neighbors in helping to finish his orders. This was a labyrinthine system.

288. Just a sample of the leading discussions are: Jeremias Prassl, Humans as a Service: The Promise and Perils of Work in the Gig Economy (2018); Catherine Ruckelshaus, Rebecca Smith, Sarah Leberstein & Eunice Cho, Who's the Boss: Restoring Accountability for Labor Standards in Outsourced Work, National Employment Law Project Report (NELP) (May 2014); Rebecca Smith & Sarah Leberstein, Rights on Demand: Ensuring Workplace Standards and Worker Security in the On-Demand Economy, (NELP Report) (Sept. 2015); Siou Chew Kuek *et al.*, The Global Opportunity in Online Outsourcing (World Bank Report) (June 2015); David Rolf, Shelby Clark & Currie Bryant, Portable Benefits in the 21st Century: Shaping a New System of Benefits for Independent Workers (Aspen Institute Report) (2016).
289. For that reason, the treatment of people working at home on a putting-out basis challenged established labor protective law. *See* Annot, *Industrial Homeworkers as Within Social Security, Unemployment Compensation, Fair Labor Standards, or Workmen's Compensation Act*, 143 ALR 418 (1943).
290. Since 2015, California law renders a "client employer"—a business that "obtains or is provided workers" from a labor contractor—a supplying entity—to perform labor in its usual course of business jointly and severally liable with the labor contractor for the payment of wages and workers' compensation coverage for workers so assigned. Cal. Lab. Code §2810.3.

### [B] Privacy

Writing in 1966, the eminent sociologist, Edward Shils, termed the last quarter of the nineteenth century the "golden age of privacy."[291] Reflecting on that observation fifty years later, this author concurred, "not because of law or inherent managerial respect, but because technology necessary for systematic intrusion was absent."[292] The development and deployment of ever more intrusive means of systematic surveillance and control of workers by technological means has burgeoned over the course of the last quarter of the twentieth century. Background checks for criminal records, which had required laborious inspection of paper courthouse records—a time consuming and expensive process—is now to be done cheaply and quickly by the click of a mouse, even as the records accessed might be no more accurate. A federal "Rap Back" system has been established whereby participating states can authorize employers to connect to the Federal Bureau of Investigation database and receive a report whenever an employee's fingerprint is registered in the system; in effect, a system of continuous monitoring for employee involvement with the criminal justice system insofar as their fingerprints are involved.[293]

Serious public attention started in the 1980s with the rise of what was then called the "electronic sweatshop"—by contemporary standards rather crude means of computerized work monitoring.[294] Today, monitoring software has extended to inventory and cash register systems that are programmed to detect possible theft or fraud—an increase in credit card sales keyed by hand, a record of refunds made by the same clerk at shift change, a persistently lower sales volume registered by a particular clerk at a particular time—all in real time.[295] Interactive badges have been deployed to record the food purchased at the company dining facility to monitor good eating habits as part of a company "wellness" program, to reduce medical insurance costs: it has been estimated that in 2018, 13 million employees have fitness trackers as part of company "wellness" programs.[296] Systems have been installed for food service and health-care workers that record whether or not an employee, who enters a restroom, has stood for a specified period of time before the sink with the water running and whether or not the soap dispenser was used.[297] Systems that instantaneously transmit "g force" events while driving to a central control, to monitor driver behavior by both electronic monitoring of engine data and video and voice recording of the driver, have been used to investigate accidents and driver behavior.[298]

---

291. Edward Shils, *Privacy: It's Constitution and Vicissitudes*, 31 L. & Contemp. Probs. 281, 292 (1966).
292. Matthew Finkin, *"Privacy: Its Constitution and Vicissitudes"—A Half Century On*, 18 Can. Lab. & Emp. L.J. 349, 358 (2015).
293. Illinois has authorized participation. 20 ILCS 2630/3.3.
294. Office of Technology Assessment, THE ELECTRONIC SUPERVISOR (1987); Shoshana Zuboff, IN THE AGE OF THE SMART MACHINE: THE FUTURE OF WORK AND POWER (1984).
295. Jennifer Lee, *Tracking Sales and the Cashiers*, N.Y. TIMES, July 11, 2001, at C-1.
296. *Technology: Wearables in the Workplace—A New Frontier*, 101 DLR (BNA) (May 24, 2018).
297. *Did Workers Wash? High-Tech Gizmo Checks*, ST. LOUIS POST-DISPATCH, Aug. 31, 1997 (from the Washington Post).
298. *See, e.g.*, http://www.drivecam.com/our-company/about-drivecam.

The technology has been deployed to monitor a person's presence in geographic space[299] and over time. Google has announced a product—Google Map Coordinate—that couples its map product to smartphones that will allow an employer to create a real-time record of worker location, even inside a building.[300] Biometric technology is being deployed apace, thus far, for control of access to the workplace and for time-keeping purposes. A February 2018, poll of 492 IT professionals in North America and Europe conducted by Spiceworks, a professional network for the IT, indicated that 62% of the respondents' companies used biometrics: of these, 57% used fingerprint scanners, 14% used facial recognition, 5% used hand geometry recognition, 3% iris scanning, 2% voice recognition, 2% palm-vein recognition.[301]

The collection, collation, and manipulation of large bodies of information—the deployment of means of technological oversight and control—threaten to erode or possibly destroy values that many believe inhere in the worker's very humanity and are essential to social wellbeing.[302] The more ubiquitous the technology's deployment, the greater might be the societal consequences, not all or even much of which can now with clarity be foreseen. Importantly, the protection of worker privacy stands out from all the other persistent and emerging issues discussed above by the fact that it does not fall with particular force on the low waged. The fact, the more affluent and powerful may be more greatly affected; but, as Shils observed, these are much the same people who invade privacy—in the name corporate profits, governmental oversight, or social science research. Suffice it to say, the legal issues are new and challenging. American law is barely coming to grapple with them.

299. *Cf.* A.H. v. Northside Indep. School Dist., 916 F. Supp. 2d 757 (W.D. Tex. 2013) (on the constitutionality of requiring students to carry "Smart ID's" containing RFID location chips).

300. Quentin Hardy, *Google Maps Where Your Workers Are*, N.Y. TIMES BITS [THE BUSINESS OF TECHNOLOGY] (June 21, 2012); Thomas Claburn, *Google Maps Coordinate App Connects Mobile Workers*, *available at* http://www.informationweek.com/news/smb/mobile/240002512 (June 22, 2012).

301. Roy Maurer, *More Employers Are Using Biometric Authentication*, Society for Human Resource Management (Apr. 6, 2018).

302. The literature on privacy—in philosophy, history, sociology, and law—is daunting. Some, but only some of the major English language sources are set out in the *Introduction* to Matthew Finkin, PRIVACY IN EMPLOYMENT LAW xxxvii-xxxv (5th ed. 2018). The issue of privacy has had deeper legal address in Europe. *See* Frank Hendrickx, EMPLOYMENT PRIVACY LAW IN THE EUROPEAN UNION: SURVEILLANCE AND MONITORING (2002) and Frank Hendrickx, EMPLOYMENT PRIVACY LAW IN THE EUROPEAN UNION: HUMAN RESOURCES AND SENSITIVE DATA (2003).

# CHAPTER 6
# The Labor Question's Third Century

The Labor Question in America, foreshadowed in the protests of the 1830s, took on urgency with industrialization and culminated in a solution in the 1930s: citizenship would become embodied in economic participation; collective representation would become a critical component of economic citizenship. Over time, the former took firm root. The latter has withered leaving workplace problems to be dealt with by law instead of collective workplace engagement howsoever problematic the law might be in implementation. All this has been canvassed above.

Whether and which aspects of waged labor raise genuinely new problems has percolated throughout this lecture. One question that has not yet been mentioned is the consequence of the emphasis America has placed on educational attainment, in particular a four-year college degree, as key to meaningful economic participation. College graduates tend to earn more and to be less susceptible to long-term unemployment than those lacking that credential. Nevertheless, some have discerned a negative effect: that college degrees are being required for jobs for which that level of attainment is not necessary. Almost two decades ago, Pryor and Schaffer argued that

> fewer jobs for prime-age workers in high levels of education have opened up than those possessing the requisite educational requirements. At the same time, more jobs have opened up for those with few educational qualifications than those workers having the corresponding level of education. As a result, an important downward occupational mobility has taken place, so that workers with more education are displacing those with less education. That is, these more-educated workers are holding jobs for which they are educationally overqualified and, as a result, much of the educational upgrading is apparent rather than real.[303]

303. Frederic Pryor & David Schaffer, WHO'S NOT WORKING AND WHY: EMPLOYMENT, COGNITIVE SKILLS, WAGES, AND THE CHANGING U.S. LABOR MARKET 45 (1999).

As a result, overqualified job takers feel themselves underrewarded and underemployed.[304] This question was raised almost fifty years ago.[305] It has resurged.

What remains to be attended to is The Labor Problem in its third century, circa 2030. Close observers of current trends have focused on the consequences of the deployment of technology to the content and, perhaps, the very existence of jobs. As we have seen, this is not new. The consequences of machine production were pointed to as a labor question in the Gilded Age. Henry Booth termed it "revolutionary." John Swinton spoke of it as "the most serious problem that has ever confronted mankind." Both were concerned about the permanent replacement of labor by machines—to Swinton only manual labor, to Booth "thinking" labor as well.[306] That issue has resurfaced since in two waves.

## §6.01 TECHNOLOGY AND JOBS

"Popular concerns about the employment effects of technological change had arisen for decades before the 1920s."[307] But in the late 1920s and early 30s, and then, again, in the 1960s, it became a subject of intense debate among economists—in the former period debating "technological unemployment," in the latter debating a broader notion of "structural unemployment." In the former period, Rexford Tugwell saw the nation as in a period of unprecedented progress, if not quite "a new industrial revolution."[308] Because of the enormous advances in productivity afforded by machines he offered a few "practical suggestions" one of which was "That machinery be made to work for us longer and faster than it characteristically does," to reduce the hours of work down to four hours a day.[309] He urged that as industry "comes of age" we should "socialize industry," to make it serve "social ends rather than individual ones."[310] The public debate on this new industrial revolution ended with the Second World War.

---

304. Jaison Abel, Richard Deitz & Yaquin Su, *Are Recent College Graduates Finding Good Jobs?*, 20 Fed. Reserve Bank of N.Y., Current Issues 1 (2014); *see also More College Graduates Finding Work, but Not in Best Jobs, Data Show*, 67 DLR (Apr. 7, 2016) at A-10 (reporting that almost 45% of new graduates took jobs that typically did not require a degree); Burningglass Technologies, Moving the Goal Posts: How Demand for a Bachelor's Degree in Reshaping the Workforce 2 (Sept. 2014) (evidence "suggests that employers may be relying on a B.A. as a broad recruitment filter that may or may not correspond to specific capabilities needed to do the job.").
305. Ivar Berg, EDUCATION AND JOBS: THE GREAT TRAINING ROBBERY (1971).
306. Swinton, *supra* n. 32. Booth, *supra* n. 31. As Booth put it:

> From the simplest tools in common use to the most complicated machine, whereby man has contrived to make matter do everything but think, and has even dispensed with the necessity for doing that, the triumphs of human skill have been most marvelous.

307. Gregory Woirol, THE TECHNOLOGICAL UNEMPLOYMENT AND STRUCTURAL UNEMPLOYMENT DEBATES 26 (1996).
308. Rexford Tugwell, INDUSTRY'S COMING OF AGE 26 (1927).
309. *Id.* at 222-23.
310. *Id.* at 230-31.

Starting in the 1950s, industry began to introduce machinery that freed the flow of production from human control. This was called "automation."[311] As in the 20s, a fierce debate ensued some insisting that automation was different from past technological change,[312] that this time there actually was a "Second Industrial Revolution"[313] that it would create new specialties and more high skilled jobs[314]; it would displace semi-skilled factory operatives. "[T]hose who work in the future will have more leisure than workers do today."[315] Those displaced "will move to other sectors of economy where their relatively low-skill level will still be wanted,"[316] or will have to be retrained.[317] Illustration 5, published in 1961, puts an ironic twist on public perception at the time.

311. AUTOMATIC CONTROL (Scientific American Editors 1955).
312. Woirol, *supra* n. 307 at 103.
313. Robert Dubin, THE WORLD OF WORK Ch. 11 (1958) (summarizing the state of the literature). Robert Heilbroner was skeptical of the claims made for the consequences of automation. Robert Heilbroner, *Men and machines in perspective* in THE TRIPLE REVOLUTION 27 (1964). He stressed that what was involved was limited to industrial manufacture which had declined in labor market significance while services look the lion's share of the labor market. He did not see any reason *a priori* why a dollar's worth of automated equipment should replace labor any more than a dollar's worth of any other piece of equipment. However, he did see new technology—he mentioned computers—as threatening a whole group of skills: sorting, filing, calculating, and "remembering." *Id.* at 33-34.
314. George Schulz & George Baldwin, AUTOMATION: A NEW DIMENSION TO OLD PROBLEMS 12 (1955) ("[W]e may well see ... a further reduction in the number of unskilled jobs and an increase in emphasis on the more skilled and professional occupations.")
315. Dubin, *supra* n. 313 at 208.
316. *Id.* at 201.
317. *Id.* ("The retraining problem entails large financial burdens. It also means great human costs to those who are displaced from their regular jobs.") *See also* Schultz & Baldwin, *supra* n. 314 at 20. ("The major social problem connected with automation—displacement of labor—is almost certain to bring with it increased emphasis on means of cushioning the shock to the worker and of retraining him to a useful and satisfying economic role of our society.")

**Illustration 5**

"BUT, SIR, YOU TOLD US SENTIMENT MUSTN'T STOP AUTOMATION."

Permission to reprint by the St. Louis Post-Dispatch Editorial Cartoon Collection, The State Historical Society of Missouri, Manuscript Collection.

The thought that work done by machines would relieve man of the need to labor has deep historical resonance, from Aristotle's *Politics* in the fourth century BCE to Keynes rumination on *Economic Possibilities for Our Grandchildren* in 1930 with much in between.[318] In the 1960s, the prospect of "too much" leisure generated by increased

318. *See* THE OXFORD BOOK OF WORK 577-583 (Keith Thomas, ed. 1999).

productivity was taken seriously.[319] The Twentieth Century Fund commissioned a study of the consequences of so much free time by the political scientist and philosopher Sebastian de Grazia. He observed that, "There will either be the same number of jobs—but with their hours cut down drastically and legislation to prevent overtime and moonlighting—or, more likely in view of the first possibility, a relative few will work, and the rest will live on Easy Street."[320] This debate ended with the Vietnam War.[321]

A half century on the deployment of technology to render existing jobs obsolete while creating new ones in an incessant drive toward ever greater productivity is simply assumed as a matter of course.[322] As in the 1930s, creative destruction is seen as an historical companion of capitalism with little fuss to be made about it.[323] After all, the manufacture of glass, ceramics, and textiles in late eighteenth century England needed alkali which, at the time, was derived from burning kelp. When, in the early nineteenth century, alkali could be produced industrially, thousands of Scottish kelp workers became unemployed.[324] We are not told what happened to them even as jobs were surely created for chemists and workers in alkali manufacture. In 1910, there were over sixty-three thousand hostlers and stable hands in the U.S., predominantly employed in horse-drawn urban transportation.[325] The training and care of horses was skilled work.[326] But, the electrification of street rail transport eliminated the need for hostlers even as it created jobs "such as electricians, linemen, and powerhouse workers which more than made up for job losses in the obsolete horse stables."[327] We are not told what happened to the hostlers. In 1900, there were over 60,000 "telegraph operators."[328] The job no longer exists.

## §6.02 IS THIS TIME DIFFERENT?

The argument today turns to the impact of far more sophisticated information technology and robotization, to "artificial intelligence (AI),"[329] the development and deployment of machines capable of learning and acting interactively with other machines largely independent of human supervision or control. This technology

319. Herbert Simon, THE SHAPE OF AUTOMATION 4-6 (1965). ("A Glut of Goods and Leisure").
320. Sebastian de Grazia, OF TIME, WORK, AND LEISURE 329 (1962) (references omitted).
321. Woirol, *supra* n. 307 at 127.
322. *See generally*, Pierre Cahuc & André Zylberberg, THE NATURAL SURVIVAL OF WORK: JOB CREATION AND JOB DESTRUCTION IN A GROWING ECONOMY (William McCraig, trans. 2006).
323. Lyon et al., *supra* n. 132.
324. Jenny Uglow, THE LUNAR MEN 159-161 (2002).
325. Bureau of Census, IV THIRTEENTH CENSUS OF THE UNITED STATES TAKEN IN THE YEAR 1910, 53 (1914).
326. Scott Malloy, TROLLY WARS: STREET CAR WORKERS ON THE LINE 63 (1996).
327. *Id.* at 79.
328. Edwin Gabler, THE AMERICAN TELEGRAPHER: A SOCIAL HISTORY, 1860-1900, Table 4.1 at 109 (1988).
329. In private conversation, a good friend, an internationally prominent British physicist, derided the phrase. "Look here," he said, "if someone came to you with a hundred thousand photographs of cats and asked you to develop an algorithm that would discern the essence of catness you'd tell him to go to hell and go to a pub. *That's* an intelligent response."

already has and is likely to continue to displace some forms of work[330] and to challenge the conditions physical and emotional of those who work with or might be supervised, or even evaluated by machines. Effort is being put to inquire into what the future might hold,[331] to what current trends are and what they might portend. Contemporary concern is captured in Illustration 6, published in 2017. Note the echo with the concerns expressed fifty years ago captured in Illustration 5.

**Illustration 6**

Reprinted with the permission of Steve Breen, the San Diego Tribune, creators.com.

Regarding the longer term, in 2016, the Organization for Economic Co-Operation and Development (OECD) projected the percentage of workers deemed at "high risk" and "significant risk" of being automated across a range of developed countries. In the U.S., 8% of employees were thought to hold jobs at high risk and another 26% at significant risk;[332] that is, over a third of the workforce is at high or significant risk of displacement.

330. *E.g.*, Jerry Kaplan, Humans Need Not Apply: A Guide to Wealth and Work in the Age of Artificial Intelligence (2015); Martin Ford, Rise of the Robots: Technology and the Threat of a Jobless Future (2015); Erik Brynjolfsson & Andrew McAfee, The Second Machine Age: Work, Progress, and Prosperity in a Time of Brilliant Technologies (2014); Simon Head, The New Ruthless Economy: Work and Power in the Digital Age (2003). *Special Report: Artificial Intelligence*, 419 The Economist (June 25, 2016).

331. World Economic Forum, Eight Futures of Work 6 (Jan. 2018) ("[M]any in the workforce ... face a rapidly shrinking field of opportunities as their skill sets have been deemed largely redundant.")

332. OECD, Employment Outlook 2016, Box 2.3 at p. 78.

PricewaterhouseCoopers has further refined how the rollout of technology is likely to affect the composition of jobs. The impact, as it sees it, is likely to unfold into the 2030s in three overlapping waves.[333] Its report assesses the degree of risk by job and industry depending on the "wave", that is the nature of the process resulting in displacement. The conclusions, though more fine grained, are concordant with the OECD's, of about 40% job displacement.

A McKinsey & Company report considered the replacement of skills, not jobs. It concluded that only about 5% of occupations were susceptible to "full automation," but that about half of the activities people are paid to do were susceptible to automation by currently demonstrated techniques.[334] Though automation has disproportionately affected middle-skill workers, it opined that both low and high skilled work would become more susceptible to automation.[335]

To similar effect, a Morgan Stanley research group took up the impact of robotic process automation on business processing outsourcing. It concluded that white collar jobs could be lost in much the same range, "not only jobs with routine/repetitive tasks ... but AI also puts [at risk] jobs involving cognitive skills at work, although the probability is lower ... ."[336]

David Autor and Anna Salmons conclude that productivity growth, which robotization and information technology promises, will add to employment in the aggregate; but, consistent with the story of job polarization, the jobs added will be bimodally distributed: the jobs retained or created will be those most resistant to machine displacement, that is, well-paid high skilled jobs and low paid low-skill jobs.[337]

There is more in the picture. The U.S. has experienced a decline in the labor market participation rate, of people who neither hold nor look for a job, since the 1960s, especially among the cohort of "prime-age" men, those between 25 and 54 years

---

333. PWC, Will robots really steal our jobs? An international analysis of the potential long-term impact of automation (Jan. 2018). The "waves" are:

    1. **Algorithm wave**: focused on automation of simple computational tasks and analysis of structured data in areas like finance, information and communications—this is already well underway.
    2. **Augmentation wave**: focused on automation of repeatable tasks such as filling in forms, communicating and exchanging information through dynamic technological support, and statistical analysis of unstructured data in semi-controlled environments such as aerial drones and robots in warehouses—this is also underway, but is likely to come to full majority in the 2020s.
    3. **Autonomy wave**: focused on automation of physical labour and manual dexterity, and problem solving in dynamic real-world situations that require responsive actions, such as in manufacturing and transport (e.g. driverless vehicles)—these technologies are under development already, but may only come to full maturity on an economy-wide scale in the 2030s.

334. McKinsey Global Institute, A Future that Works: Automation, Employment, and Productivity 1 (Jan. 2017).
335. *Id.* p. 2.
336. Morgan Stanley Research, Process Automation: The Rise of the Machines 46 (Sept. 24, 2017).
337. David Autor & Anna Salomens, Does Productivity Growth Threaten Employment? "Robocalypse Now?", (European Central Bank Annual Conference Paper) (June 27, 2017). This is concordant with earlier predictions. Michael Katz & Mark Stern, One Nation Divisible: What America Was and What It Is Becoming 179-181 (2006).

of age: from a participation rate of 91.8% in 1966 to 88.6% today—from 4.6 to 7.1 million men—which decline accelerated over the past two decades.[338] Didem Tüzemon, an economist with the Federal Reserve Bank of Kansas City, attributes the decline to job polarization: that "declining demand for middle-skill workers in response to advancements in technology and globalization, has been a key contributor to the increase in nonparticipation among prime-age men."[339] The largest increase in labor market nonparticipation was among those men with a middle level of education, that is those with a high school degree and some college education, perhaps a two-year associate degree. Middle-skill jobs more often consist of routine, rule-based work.

Tasks performed in high- and low-skill jobs, however, are more difficult to automate, making them "nonroutine" jobs. Workers in low-skill jobs typically have lower educational attainment and work in jobs that are physically demanding. Many of these jobs are service oriented, such as food preparation, cleaning, and security and protective services. In contrast, workers in high-skill jobs are typically highly educated and perform tasks requiring analytical ability, problem-solving, and creativity. Many of these jobs are managerial, professional, and technical in nature in fields such as engineering, finance, management, and medicine.[340]

In 2017, the National Academies of Science, Engineering, and Medicine published a study of the direction and impact of information technology on the American workforce. The study is upbeat in terms of macroeconomic impact, concordant with Autor and Salmons and others. Of the impact of technology on work it observed:

> First and foremost, work provides income and economic stability. Jobs enable parents to feed, house, and educate their children. At their best, jobs also employ and cultivate our skills and strengths, provide community, and enable us to contribute to society. Jobs can shape individuals' identities and help provide a sense of meaning or purpose.[341]

---

338. Didem Tüzemen, *Why Are Prime-Age Men Vanishing from the Labor Force?* 103 Econ. Rev. 5 (2018).
339. *Id.* at 6. According to the most recent Bureau of Labor Statistics data, even as the economy's robust recovery has reduced the unemployment rate—those seeking a job—to a fifty year low of 3.7%, prime age male labor market participation increased by only 0.4%, that is, to a prime age male labor market participation rate of 89%.
340. *Id.* at 18. Alan Krueger has looked at the same cohort through a different lens and came to the dispiriting conclusion that fully half of prime-age men not participating in the labor market take pain medication on a daily basis—two thirds of them take prescription medication—and that 40% reported that their pain prevented them from working in a full-time job. Alan B. Krueger, Where Have All the Workers Gone? An Inquiry into the Decline of the U.S. Labor Force Participating Rate, (Brookings Papers on Economic Activity) (2017). Of this, Tüzemon observes that "it is hard to know whether these men left the labor force because of a disability that required pain medication or whether they became dependent on pain medication because they were forced out of the labor force for other reasons." Tüzemon *supra* n. 338 at 16. He goes on: "Some anecdotal evidence suggests individuals are likely to claim disability when they are unable to find new jobs after losing their jobs." *Id.* (reference omitted.) Recent data indicates a significant up-tick in the employment of the disabled. "On the other hand, over the last three and a half years, their wages have been 16 percent lower on average than those of other new job finders." Ernie Tedeschi, *Disabled Workers Offer Labor Clues*, N.Y. Times, Mar. 17, 2018 at B-5.
341. National Academes of Sciences, Information Technology, and the U.S. Workforce: Where Are We and Where Do We Go From Here? 16 (2017).

As did students of automation in the 60s, the report dwelled on the role of education, especially in an education "that prepares the workforce for future dynamism in employment opportunities and enables lifelong learning,"[342] "enabling flexibility in the face of changing circumstances will likely be important."[343] Unlike the 60s, however, the report makes scant mention of what should be done about those whose skills have been rendered obsolete in the short term, especially those with middle skills and modest educational attainment who, we are told, are most susceptible to job displacement and for whom "lifelong learning" in future offers no prospect in the here and now.[344] The velocity of displacement may determine how pressured America will be to retrain,[345] but the Academies' report elides the subject, possibly because of America's rather dismal record in worker retraining,[346] this to echo Gregory Woirol's comment on the technological unemployment debates of the past: "Economists who were concerned about the details of the adjustment process because of the time involved or the extent of displacement effects had a difficult time convincing their colleagues that there was an issue worth worrying about."[347] Or, perhaps, the worry should not be about retraining, but about matching employers with those who already have the skills they need or who can be brought up to speed easily.[348]

As we reach the point of The Labor Question's third century is there something to worry about? From what we have been given to understand so far, two non-competing narratives are presented, both projecting out current trends: (1) accelerating bi-modal distribution of workers as creative destruction abetted by technology proceeds apace; and, (2) increasing labor market nonparticipation for want of jobs workers are willing or, in some cases, equipped to work.

### [A] Greater Inequality

Now, as in the past, those who have been displaced by technology and who have or can attain the skills needed in an automated, roboticized, and computerized world of work will find jobs; those displaced who either lack needed skills or cannot acquire them will either find employment compatible with what they can offer or cease labor market participation. In the longer run this should not be a labor problem for inevitably those

342. *Id.* at 113.
343. *Id.* at 114. *See also* Finding No. 5 on adaptation of the educational system in future. *Id.* at 140.
344. The earlier emphasis on retraining has been reiterated today. *E.g.* World Economic Forum, Towards a Reskilling Revolution: A Future of Jobs for All (Jan. 2018); *Special Report: Lifelong Learning*, 422 The Economist (Jan. 14, 2017). But the extent to which workers with middle level skills and modest levels of education can be retrained for well-paid jobs remains to be seen.
345. Schultz & Baldwin, *supra* n. 314, made that point; but they laid great stress on the role of unions in negotiating for the retraining of those displaced. That approach has been taken off the table with union implosion.
346. Kathleen Thelen, Varieties of Liberalization and the New Politics of Social Solidarity 75-85 (2014).
347. Woirol, *supra* n. 307 at 144.
348. Andrew Weaver & Paul Osterman, *Skill Demand and Mismatch in U.S. Manufacturing*, 70 ILR Rev. 275 (2017).

displaced will exit the scene[349]; and if their successors have been better fitted for the vicissitudes of an ever-changing labor market, displacement should have only modest effects. This scenario elides the nature of the jobs that will be available to displaced workers.

Because the labor market will have become more polarized, the working force will be more divided between the well-paid high skilled and the low paid low skilled, though it was noted earlier that advancing technology might well flatten this out in time. In the short to medium term, the situation of the low waged in future promises to extend the labor problems facing the low waged today, unless redressed in the interim: their income and hours will be precarious; they will lack collective representation; they will be incapable of enforcing whatever protective law might theoretically apply

349. This opens up the complex set of issues surrounding the aging of the American population. There is too much to be taken up here. A good introduction is supplied by Anne Alstott, A NEW DEAL FOR OLD AGE: TOWARD A PROGRESSIVE RETIREMENT (2016). It is enough to note that since the post-War period ushered in the notion of retirement, a worker's ability to retire with an adequate income was dependent on three elements—social security, savings, and an employer-provided pension. Social security is under significant demographic pressure; fewer employees have employer-sponsored pensions and even these have shifted to money purchase plans from guaranteed benefit plans, often non-contributory by the employer as the figure below evidences.

*Share of Pension Participants in Defined-Contribution and Defined-Benefit Plans, 1980-2004*

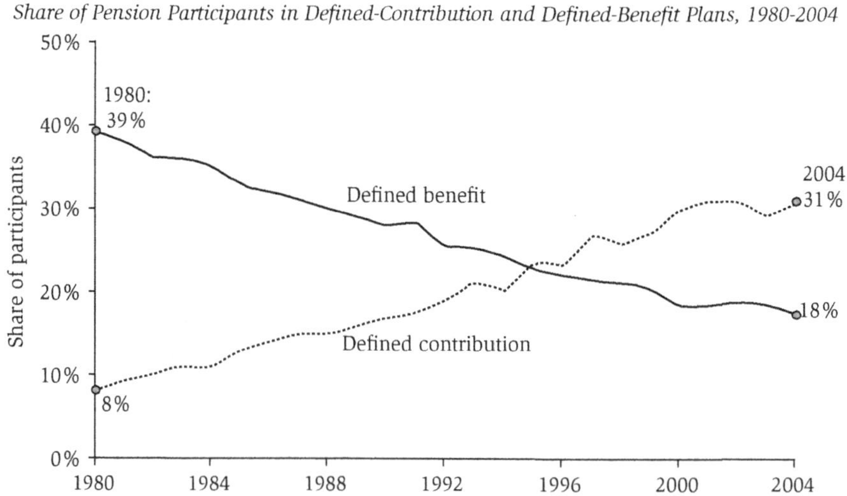


*Source*: THE STATE OF WORKING AMERICA, *supra*, Figure 4.11. Note: Data are for private sector workers.

As for savings, in 2016, the median household led by a person 65 or older had $60,000 in savings, the bottom 25% had saved at most $3,260. Tara Siegel Bernard, *Bankruptcy Booms Among Older Americans as Safety Net Frays*, N.Y. Times (Aug. 6, 2018) at pp. A-1, A-11.

because the hearing of their claims will have been subsumed into atomized arbitration. Many will be classified as self-employed, depriving them of even the nominal rights "employees" have, especially those working in the on-demand economy to which the attribution of pre-industrial independent proprietorship would be *une mauvaise plaisanterie,*[350] though some might use their status as small businesses as a basis to pursue such statutory or common law protections as might be made to apply. Those working at the higher end would continue to confront extant labor problems—of discrimination, restrictions on mobility, and wrongful dismissal, for example—as well as the further development of currently nascent issues of ownership or control of intellectual property.[351]

### [B] Opting Out

The complementary narrative,[352] hinted at in the studies of labor market nonparticipation by prime-age men, is that of the emergence of a society whose prime-age population includes a rising cohort of those who are able to but do not and do not expect to engage in a waged work career, a cohort incrementally larger than today's 11.4% prime-age nonparticipation rate. Perhaps 15%? More?

The Academies' study considered work almost exclusively in economic terms;[353] but, as Sebastian de Grazia noted when the impact of automation was being seriously debated a half century ago, government might guarantee pay without jobs. The idea would not be new. One Nathaniel Sellick, appearing before the Hewitt Committee, a Congressional investigation into the "The Great Problem" in 1878, proposed that the federal government "give everybody $58."[354] Serious proposals for a basic income paid to all are being essayed today.[355]

350. Andrew Haldane, Chief Economist of the Bank of England, opined that there are parallels between modern on-demand labor market practices and pre-industrial ones. Andrew Haldane, Work, Wages and Monetary Policy (June 20, 2017) (available at www.bankofengland.co.uk/ speeches). Ilana Gershon has observed that high-end employees are encouraged to conceive of and present themselves as businesses offering to solve business problems in the short term even as they are ever on the lookout for another job, that is another short-term business relationship. Ilana Gershon, Down and Out in the New Economy: How People Find (or Don't Find) Work Today (2017).

351. The essential background to which is supplied by Catherine Fisk, Working Knowledge: Employee Innovation and the Rise of Corporate Intellectual Property, 1800-1930 (2009).

352. Randall Collins has argued to another scenario: the collapse of capitalism. Marx predicted that capitalism would implode due of the lack of purchasing power by a working class displaced by machinery. But capitalism saved itself that fate by creating a middle class whose purchasing power sustained it. Once the middle class is hollowed out by information technology there would be little left to sustain capitalism. This scenario, he suggests, would play out by the year 2040. Randall Collins, *The End of Middle-Class Work: No More Escapes*, in Does Capitalism Have a Future? (Immanuel Wallerstein et al. eds. 2013).

353. However, the report noted in passing, that, "Work occupies a great deal of people's time and attention and has played a central role in shaping worth and identity." Academies, *supra* n. 341 at 102.

354. *Where Wise Men Pause, The Great Problem of the Time Solved Instantly*, N.Y. Times (Aug. 7, 1878). Mr. Sellicker was characterized in the news account as a man "whose business at present was trying to get business."

355. This has drawn the attention of economists, Philippe Van Parjis & Yannick Vanderborght, Basic Income: A Radical Proposal for a Free and a Sane Society (2017) and Guy Standing, Basic Income (2017), and nonspecialists, *e.g.* Andy Stern, Raising the Floor (2016).

Assuming the provision of income to everyone irrespective of whether they are engaged in waged work is economically feasible,[356] de Grazia argued to a socially problematic feature of rendering work economically inconsequential:

> If machines, tended by a few machine-herders, do the work, why should men work? The heat is off. Though we may deny that the gospel of work ever extended to miners and factory workers, the sense of national purpose work gave to all classes cannot be so easily disputed. Though we were disposed to argue, along the lines of those who say that after all the only thing the worker works for is the many mouths at home, even this motive for work is gone.[357]

356. A forthcoming number of the *Comparative Labor Law & Policy Journal* will be devoted to a discussion of these books.
357. de Grazia, *supra* n. 320 at 384.

## CHAPTER 7

# The Basis of Citizenship

In the 1830s, the mark of citizenship was a proprietary independence that discounted the status of waged work as a permanent station in life. By the late 1930s, the mark of citizenship had become identified with being a waged worker with the job security, job protections, and relative independence that unionization afforded. Under today's reigning ideology, it is job holding alone that "allows us to become fully fledged and respected communal beings" irrespective of these antecedent attributes of economic citizenship.[358] The powerfully equalitarian labor rhetoric of post-Revolutionary American strikes the modern ear as discordant, even quaint.

If, into this state of affairs, automation and information technology are deployed in such a way as to produce a nontrivial population of prime-age labor market nonparticipants, and if the state sustains that class, as it currently does the working poor, not by a web of tax credits and benefits conditioned on being waged workers or seeking so to be, but by a guaranteed income without connection to labor market participation, what becomes of economic citizenship as the "national purpose"?

The U.S. has become so work centered that individual worth and identity are inextricably bound up in having a job. Holding a job often means "better health, greater self-esteem, a favorable social status, opportunities for friendship, membership in a community, opportunities for professional and personal growth, and the sense of participating in a larger society,"[359] as well as income. So ingrained has job holding become as an element citizenship that the President's Council of Economic Advisors has sought to add a work requirement for eligibility for several welfare benefits for the poor that currently are uncoupled to waged work—to ensure that "those society

358. Brian O'Connor, IDLENESS: A PHILOSOPHICAL ESSAY 61 (2018).
359. Steven Davis, John Haltiwanger & Scott Schuh, JOB CREATION AND DESTRUCTION 156 (1998).

expects to work actually do so."[360] As things stand now, "The ethical lines have been drawn: are you a worker or a shirker?"[361]

Thus is the problem posed: what defines citizenship in a society when a good part of it has no such anchor for self-regard either their own or in the eyes of others? The philosophical quandary points to an "implausible ... scenario in which the phenomena of usefulness, competitive social identities, or long-term discipline [would] no longer form the outlines of our experience."[362] It poses a political quandary as well. Assuming that some conception of citizenship other than proprietary independence or market participation could be fashioned, can a society currently so work centered arrive at it?[363] That might become The Labor Question in this century and, if history is a guide, to take a century to sort out.

---

360. The Council of Economic Advances, Expanding Welfare Requirements in Non-cash Welfare Programs 30 (July 2018).
361. David Frayne, The Refusal of Work 16 (2015): For managers and professionals, the loss of a job can be devastating to self-worth. Kathleen Newman, Falling from Grace: Downward Mobility in the Age of Affluence (1999). This may be less likely to be so of blue collar workers. Ofer Sharone, Flawed System/Flawed Self: Job Searching and Unemployment Experiences Ch. 6 (2014).
362. O'Connor, *supra* n. 358 at 186.
363. The history of the idea of work in the Western tradition is fraught with contradiction. Work could be a curse: "By the sweat of your brow/Shall you get bread to eat." Genesis 3:19. Or a vanity: "all hard work and skill are merely man's rivalry with his neighbor." Ecclesiastes 4:4. In either case, we are well to be rid of it. But work could be a source of personal satisfaction. "Whatever is in your power to do, do it with all your might." Ecclesiastes 9:10. Fitting waged work into a scheme justifying human existence has long vexed. *E.g.* Richard Donkin, Blood Sweat & Tears: The Evolution of Work 327 (2001):

> Work and leisure are vital ingredients in the soup of life. They can run together as a single fulfilling experience. This is what should inform our ambitions—a varying flow of experience, barely separable as work or play, not the telephone-number salary.

A basic income, it is said, might free us of the former and give greater play for the latter. QED.

## BCLR - BULLETIN OF COMPARATIVE LABOUR RELATIONS

Vol. Author/Title/Year/ISBN

1. Roger Blanpain, *Individual Employment Contracts: Collective Agreements,* 1970.
2. Roger Blanpain, *Social Planning,* 1971 (ISBN 90-312-0018-2).
3. Roger Blanpain, *Guaranteed Income Funds,* 1972 (ISBN 90-312-0019-0).
4. Roger Blanpain, *Employee Participation at the Level of the Enterprise,* 1973 (ISBN 90-312-0020-4).
5. Roger Blanpain, *Vastheid van Betrekking: Staking en Bezetting,* 1974.
6. Roger Blanpain, *Labour Law and Industrial Relations (International Bibliography),* 1975 (ISBN 90-312-0023-9).
7. Roger Blanpain, *Multinational Enterprises,* 1976 (ISBN 90-312-0024-7).
8. Roger Blanpain, *Worker's Participation in the European Company,* 1977 (ISBN 90-312-0044-1).
9. Roger Blanpain, *Women and Labour,* 1978 (ISBN 90-312-0077-8).
10. Roger Blanpain, *European Conference on Labour Law and Industrial Relations: Multinational Enterprises,* 1979 (ISBN 90-312-0091-3).
11. Roger Blanpain, *Job Security and Industrial Relations,* 1980 (ISBN 90-312-0147-2).
12. Roger Blanpain, Greg Bamber & Russell Lansbury, *Technological Change and Industrial Relations: An International Symposium,* 1983 (ISBN 90-312-0205-3).
13. Roger Blanpain, James Janssen van Raay & A. Moulty, *Worker's Participation in the European Community: The Fifth Directive,* 1984 (ISBN 90-654-4187-5).
14. Roger Blanpain, *Equality and Prohibition of Discrimination in Employment,* 1985 (ISBN 90-654-4215-4).
15. Roger Blanpain, *Restructuring Labour in the Enterprise: Law and Practice in France, F.R. of Germany, Italy, Sweden and the United Kingdom,* 1986 (ISBN 90-654-4283-9).
16. Roger Blanpain & E. Kassalow, *Unions and Industrial Relations: Recent Trends and Prospect: A Comparative Treatment,* 1987 (ISBN 90-654-4294-4).
17. Roger Blanpain & Marco Biagi, *Trade Union Democracy and Industrial Relations,* 1988 (ISBN 90-654-4394-0).
18. Roger Blanpain & Jelle Visser, *In Search of Inclusive Unionism,* 1990 (ISBN 90-654-4439-4).
19. Roger Blanpain, *Flexibility and Wages: A Comparative Treatment,* 1990 (ISBN 90-654-4461-0).

20. Roger Blanpain, Stephen Frenkel & Oliver Clarke, *Economic Restructuring and Industrial Relations in Industrialised Countries,* 1990 (ISBN 90-654-4488-2).
21. Roger Blanpain & Friedrich Fürstenberg, *Structure and Strategy in Industrial Relations,* 1991 (ISBN 90-654-4559-5).
22. Roger Blanpain, Amira Galin & Ozer Carmi, *Flexible Work Patterns and Their Impact on Industrial Relations,* 1991 (ISBN 90-654-4572-2).
23. Roger Blanpain, *Workers' Participation: Influence on Management Decision-Making by Labour in the Private Sector,* 1992 (ISBN 90-654-4600-1).
24. Roger Blanpain, Brian Brooks & Chris Engels, *Employed or Self-Employed,* 1992 (ISBN 90-654-4613-3).
25. Roger Blanpain & Tiziano Treu, *Industrial Relations Developments in the Telecommunications Industry,* 1993 (ISBN 90-654-4642-7).
26. Roger Blanpain & Marco Biagi, *Industrial Relations in Small and Medium Sized Enterprises,* 1993 (ISBN 90-654-4696-6).
27. Roger Blanpain & Marco Biagi, *Participative Management and Industrial Relations in a Worldwide Perspective,* 1993 (ISBN 90-654-4769-5).
28. Roger Blanpain, Jacques Rojot & Hoyt N. Wheeler, *Employee Rights and Industrial Justice,* 1994 (ISBN 90-654-4804-7).
29. Roger Blanpain & Ruth Ben-Israel, *Strikes and Lock-Outs in Industrialized Market Economies,* 1994 (ISBN 90-654-4841-1).
30. Roger Blanpain, Kazuo Sugeno & Yasuo Suwa, *The Harmonization of Working Life and Family Life,* 1995 (ISBN 90-411-0064-4).
31. Roger Blanpain & Laszio Nagy, *Labour Law and Industrial Relations in Central and Eastern Europe,* 1996 (ISBN 90-411-0298-1).
32. Roger Blanpain, *Labour Law and Industrial Relations in the European Union,* 1997 (ISBN 90-411-0527-1).
33. Taco Van Peijpe, *Employment Protection under Strain,* 1998 (ISBN 90-411-0528-8).
34. Roger Blanpain, Takashi Araki & Ryuichi Yamakawa, *The Process of Industrialization and the Role of Labour Law in Asia,* 1999 (ISBN 9-041-1104-7-X).
35. Roger Blanpain & Marco Biagi, *Non-standard Work and Industrial Relations,* 1999 (ISBN 90-411-1117-4).
36. Roger Blanpain, *Private Employment Agencies: The Impact of ILO Convention 181 (1997) and the Judgment of the European Court of Justice of 11 December 1997,* 1999 (ISBN 90-411-1118-2).
37. Roger Blanpain, *Multinational Enterprises and the Social Challenges of the XXIst Century: The ILO Declaration on Fundamental* Principles *at Work, Public and Private Corporate Codes of Conduct,* 2000 (ISBN 90-411-1280-4).
38. Roger Blanpain, Ryuichi Yamakawa & Takashi Araki, *Deregulation and Labour Law: In Search of a Labour Concept for the 21st Century,* 2000 (ISBN 90-411-1370-3).
39. Roger Blanpain, *The Council of Europe and the Social Challenges of the XXIst Century,* 2001 (ISBN 90-411-1543-9).

40. Roger Blanpain, *On-Line Rights for Employees in the Information Society, Use & Monitoring of E-Mail & Internet at Work*, 2002 (ISBN 90-411-1626-5).
41. Roger Blanpain, *The Evolving Employment Relationship and the New Economy: The Role of Labour Law & Industrial Relations*, 2001 (ISBN 90-411-1691-5).
42. Roger Blanpain, *Involvement of Employees in the European Union, Works Councils, Company Statute, Information and Consultation Rights*, 2002 (ISBN 90-411-1760-1).
43. Michele Colucci, *The Impact of the Internet and New Technologies on the Workplace: A Legal Analysis from a Comparative Point of View*, 2002 (ISBN 90-411-1824-1).
44. Roger Blanpain, *White Paper on the Labour Market in Italy: The Quality of European Industrial Relations and Changing Industrial Relations*, 2002 (ISBN 90-411-1841-1).
45. Roger Blanpain, Russell D. Lansbury & Young-Bum Park, *Impact of Globalisation on Employment Relations: A Comparison of the Automobile and Banking Industries in Australia and Korea*, 2002 (ISBN 90-411-1850-0).
46. Roger Blanpain & Antoine Jacobs, *Employee Rights in Bankruptcy:* A *Comparative-Law Assessment*, 2002 (ISBN 90-411-1942-6).
47. Roger Blanpain, Takashi Araki & Shinya Ouchi, *Corporate Restructuring and the Role of Labour Law*, 2003 (ISBN 90-411-1949-3).
48. Roger Blanpain, *Collective Bargaining, Discrimination, Social Security and European Integration*, 2003 (ISBN 90-411-2010-6).
49. Roger Blanpain & Luis Aparicio-Valdez, *Labour Relations in the Asia- Pacific Countries*, 2004 (ISBN 90-411-2239-7).
50. Roger Blanpain & Ronnie Graham, *Temporary Agency Work and the Information Society*, 2004 (ISBN 90-411-2252-4).
51. Roger Blanpain, *The Actors of Collective Bargaining: A World Report*, 2004 (ISBN 90-411-2253-2).
52. Roger Blanpain & Michele Colucci, *The Globalisation of Labour Standards: The Soft Law Track*, 2004 (ISBN 90-411-2303-2).
53. Roger Blanpain, Takashi Araki & Shinya Ouchi, *Labour Law in Motion: Diversification of the Labour Force & Terms and Conditions of Employment*, 2005 (ISBN 90-411-2315-6).
54. Roger Blanpain, *Smoking and the Workplace*, 2005 (ISBN 90-411-2325-3).
55. Roger Blanpain, *Confronting Globalization: The Quest for a Social Agenda*, 2005 (ISBN 90-411-2381-4).
56. Roger Blanpain, Thomas Blanke & Edgar Rose, *Collective Bargaining Wages in Comparative Perspective: Germany, France, the Netherlands, Sweden and the United Kingdom*, 2005 (ISBN 90-411-2388-1).
57. Roger Blanpain & Anne Numhauser-Henning, *Women in Academia & Equality Law: Aiming High - Falling Short?*, 2006 (ISBN 978-90-411-2427-6).
58. Roger Blanpain, *Freedom of Services in the European Union: Labour and Social Security Law: The Bolkestein Initiative*, 2006 (ISBN 978-90-411-2453-5).
59. Roger Blanpain, Frans Pennings & Nurhan Sural, *Flexibilisation and Modernisation of the Turkish Labour Market*, 2006 (ISBN 978-90-411-2490-X).

60. Roger Blanpain & Boel Flodgren, *Corporate and Employment Perspectives in a Global Business Environment*, 2006 (ISBN 978-90-411-2537-X).
61. Roger Blanpain, Shinya Ouchi & Takashi Araki, *Decentralizing Industrial Relations and The Role of Labor Unions and Employee Representatives*, 2007 (ISBN 978-90-411-2583-3).
62. Roger Blanpain, *European Framework Agreements and Telework: Law and Practice: A European and Comparative Study*, 2007 (ISBN 978-90-411-2560-4).
63. Roger Blanpain, Jim Kitay, Leanne Cutcher & Nick Wailes, *Globalization and Employment Relations in Retail Banking*, 2007 (ISBN 978-90-411-2620-1).
64. Roger Blanpain, Russell Lansbury, Jim Kitay, Nick Wailes & Anja Kirsch, *Globalization and Employment Relations in the Auto Assembly Industry:* A *Study of Seven Countries*, 2008 (ISBN 978-90-411-2698-6).
65. Roger Blanpain & Michele Tiraboschi, *The Global Labour Market: From Globalization to Flexicurity*, 2008 (ISBN 978-90-411-2722-8).
66. Roger Blanpain, Michele Colucci & Frank Hendrickx, *The Future of Sport in the European Union: Beyond the EU Reform Treaty and the White Paper*, 2008 (ISBN 978-90-411-2761-7).
67. Roger Blanpain, Linda Dickens, *Challenges in European Employment Relations: Employment Regulation, Trade Union Organization, Equality, Flexicurity, Training and New Approaches to Pay*, 2008 (ISBN 978-90-411-2771-6).
68. Roger Blanpain, Hiroya Nakakubo & Takashi Araki, *New Developments in Employment Discrimination Law, 2008* (ISBN 978-90-411-2782-2).
69. Roger Blanpain, Andrzej Marian wiątkowski, *The Laval and Viking Cases: Freedom of Services and Establishment v. Industrial Conflict in the European Economic Area and Russia*, 2009 (ISBN 978-90-411-2850-8).
70. Roger Blanpain, William Bromwich, Olga Rymkevich, Silvia Spattini, *The Modernization of Labour Law and Industrial Relations in a Comparative Perspective*, 2009 (ISBN 978-90-411-2865-2).
71. Roger Blanpain, Juan Pablo Landa & Brian Langille, *Employment Policies and Multilevel Governance*, 2009 (ISBN 978-90-411-2866-9).
72. Roger Blanpain, European Works Councils; *The European Directive 2009/ 38/EC of 6 May 2009, 2009* (ISBN 978-90-411-3208-6).
73. Roger Blanpain, William Bromwich, Olga Rymkevich & Silvia Spattini, *Labour Productivity, Investment in Human Capital and Youth Employment: Comparative Developments and Global Responses*, 2010 (ISBN 978-90-411-3249-9).
74. Greg J. Bamber & Philippe Pochet, *Regulating Employment Relations, Work and Labour Laws: International Comparisons between Key Countries*, 2010 (ISBN 978-90-411-3199-7). General Editor: Roger Blanpain.
75. Roger Blanpain, Desislava Nikolaeva Dimitrova, *Seafarers' Rights in the Globalized Maritime Industry*, 2010 (ISBN 978-90-411-3349-6).
76. Roger Blanpain, Hiroya Nakakubo & Takashi Araki, *Regulation of Fixed- Term Employment Contracts*, 2010 (ISBN 978-90-411-3356-4).

77. Roger Blanpain, William Bromwich, Olga Rymkevich & Iacopo Senatori, *Rethinking Corporate Governance*, 2011 (ISBN 978-90-411-3450-9).
78. Roger Blanpain & Frank Hendrickx, *Labour Law between Change and Tradition: Liber Amicorum Antoine Jacobs*, 2011 (ISBN 978-90-411-3424-0).
79. Roger Blanpain, Thomas Klebe, Marlene Schmidt & Bernd Waas, *Trade Union Rights at the Workplace*, 2012 (ISBN 978-90-411-3460-8).
80. Roger Blanpain, William Bromwich, Olga Rymkevich & Iacopo Senatori, *Labour Markets, Industrial Relations and Human Resources Management: From Recession to Recovery*, 2012 (ISBN 978-90-411-4004-3).
81. Roger Blanpain, Hiroya Nakakubo & Takashi Araki, *Systems of Employee Representation at the Enterprise: A Comparative Study*, 2012 (ISBN 978-90-411-4080-7).
82. Roger Blanpain & Frank Hendrickx, *Temporary Agency Work in the European Union and the United States*, 2013 (ISBN 978-90-411-4769-1).
83. Roger Blanpain, Toker Dereli, Y. Pınar Soykut-Sarıca & Aslı en-Tabaı, *Emerging Patterns of Work and Turkish Labour Market Challenges under Globalization: Readings on Labour and Employment Relations*, 2014 (ISBN 978-90-411-4983-1).
84. Roger Blanpain, Pablo Arellano Ortiz, Marius Olivier & Gijsbert Vonk, *Social Security and Migrant Workers: Selected Studies of Cross-border Social Security Mechanisms*, 2014 (ISBN 978-90-411-4770-7).
85. Roger Blanpain & Nikita Lyutov, *Workers' Representation in Central and Eastern Europe: Challenges and Opportunities for the Works Councils' System*, 2014 (ISBN 978-90-411-4746-2).
86. Roger Blanpain, Ulla Liukkunen & Chen Yifeng, *China and ILO Fundamental Principles and Rights at Works*, 2014 (ISBN 978-90-411-4984-8).
87. Roger Blanpain, *The Use of Languages and Employment Relations*, 2014 (ISBN 978-90-411-5606-8).
88. Roger Blanpain, Hiroya Nakakubo & Takashi Araki, *Protection of Employees' Personal Information and Privacy*, 2014 (ISBN 978-90-411-5608-2).
89. Roger Blanpain, Jan Wouters, Glenn Rayp, Laura Beke & Axel Marx, *Protecting Labour Rights in a Multi-polar Supply Chain and Mobile Global Economy*, 2015 (ISBN 978-90-411-5662-4).
90. Roger Blanpain & Stefania Marassi, *Globalization and Transnational Collective Labour Relations: International and European Framework Agreements at Company Level*, 2015 (ISBN 978-90-411-4748-6).
91. Roger Blanpain, Frank Hendrickx & Petra Herzfeld Olsson, *National Effects of the Implementation of EU Directives on Labour Migration from Third Countries*, 2016 (ISBN 978-90-411-6257-1).
92. Roger Blanpain, Frank Hendrickx & D'Arcy du Toit, *Labour Law and Social Progress: Holding the Line or Shifting the Boundaries?* 2016 (ISBN 978-90-411-6747-7).

93. Roger Blanpain & Frank Hendrickx, *Reasonable Accommodation in the Modern Workplace: Potential and Limits of the Integrative Logics of Labour Law*, 2016 (ISBN 978-90-411-6258-8).
94. Roger Blanpain, Frank Hendrickx & Bernd Waas, *New Forms of Employment in Europe*, 2016 (ISBN 978-90-411-6239-7).
95. Roger Blanpain, Frank Hendrickx, Hiroya Nakakubo & Takashi Araki, *The Notion of Employer in the Era of the Fissured Workplace: Should Labour Law Responsibilities Exceed the Boundary of the Legal Entity?*, 2017 (ISBN 978-90-411-8470-2).
96. Elena Sychenko, *Individual Labour Rights as Human Rights: The Contributions of the European Court of Human Rights to Worker's Rights Protection*, 2017 (ISBN 978-90-411-8629-4).
97. William Bromwich & Olga Rymkevich, *Improving Workplace Quality: New Perspectives and Challenges for Worker Well-Being*, 2017 (ISBN 978-90-411-8628-7).
98. Sarah De Groof, *Work-Life Balance in the Modern Workplace: Interdisciplinary Perspectives from Work-Family Research, Law and Policy*, 2017 (ISBN 978-90-411-8630-0).
99. Sylvaine Laulom, *Collective Bargaining Developments in Times of Crisis*, 2018 (ISBN 978-90-411-8999-8).
100. Frank Hendrickx & Valerio De Stefano, *Game Changers in Labour Law: Shaping the Future of Work*, 2018 (ISBN 978-90-411-9953-9).
101. Ivana Palinkaš, *The Legal and Institutional Framing of Collective Bargaining in CEE Countries: Between Europeanisation and Decentralisation*, 2018 (ISBN 978-90-411-9199-1).
102. Jeremy Waddington, *European Board-Level Employee Representation: National Variations in Influence and Power*, 2018 (ISBN 978-90-411-9202-8).
103. Jan Pichrt & Kristina Koldinská, *Labour Law and Social Protection in a Globalized World: Changing Realities in Selected Areas of Law and Policy*, 2018 (ISBN 978-94-035-0093-5).
104. Matthew W. Finkin, *American Labor and the Law: Dormant, Resurgent, and Emergent Problems*, 2019 (ISBN 978-94-035-0654-8).